30-99

Columbia University

Contributions to Education

Teachers College Series

No. 714

AMS PRESS
NEW YORK

CERTAIN BASIC TEACHER-EDUCATION POLICIES AND THEIR DEVELOP- MENT AND SIGNIFICANCE IN A SELECTED STATE

A HISTORICAL AND INTERPRETATIVE STUDY OF
CERTAIN ASPECTS OF TEACHER EDUCATION IN NEW HAMPSHIRE
WHICH REPRESENT SIGNIFICANT DEVELOPMENTS IN THE PRO-
FESSIONAL PREPARATION OF TEACHERS IN THE UNITED STATES

By HARRY ALVIN BROWN

SUBMITTED IN PARTIAL FULFILLMENT OF THE REQUIREMENTS
FOR THE DEGREE OF DOCTOR OF PHILOSOPHY IN THE
FACULTY OF PHILOSOPHY, COLUMBIA UNIVERSITY

Published with the Approval of
Professor William C. Bagley, Sponsor

BUREAU OF PUBLICATIONS
Teachers College, Columbia University
NEW YORK CITY
1937

Library of Congress Cataloging in Publication Data

Brown, Harry Alvin, 1897-1949.
    Certain basic teacher-education policies.

    Reprint of the 1937 ed., issued in series: Teachers
College, Columbia University. Contributions to education. no. 714.
    Originally presented as the author's thesis, Columbia.
    Bibliography: p.
    1. Teachers, Training of--United States. 2. Tea-
chers Training of--New Hampshire. I. Title. II. Series: Columbia University. Teachers College. Contributions to education, no. 714.
LB1715.B75 1972   370'.71'0973   73-176597
ISBN 0-404-55714-7

Reprinted by Special Arrangement with Teachers
College Press, New York, New York

From the edition of 1937, New York
First AMS edition published in 1972
Manufactured in the United States

AMS PRESS, INC.
NEW YORK, N. Y.   10003

PREFACE

THE author is deeply indebted to Professor William C. Bagley for advice and criticism in connection with this study. Professor Bagley's course, entitled "The Professional Education of Teachers," of which the author has been privileged to be a member for a year, served as the inspiration for this study.

The plan of this dissertation was formulated in Professor E. H. Reisner's course entitled "Historical Research in American Education." Professor Reisner's stimulating criticisms in connection with another similar and related piece of historical research have been of great value in this study.

To Professor R. Bruce Raup the author is indebted for a stimulating course entitled "Foundations of Research Method." A second course taken under Professor Raup, which dealt with the philosophy of teacher education, enlarged the author's thinking in connection with curricula and procedures in the preparation of teachers.

Dr. E. W. Butterfield, Commissioner of Education in Connecticut, former Commissioner of Education in New Hampshire, has read and criticized the manuscript. He also has verified all statements concerning teacher education during his administration in New Hampshire. In an earlier period when both he and the author were engaged in public school work and later when at the same time they were members of the state department of education in New Hampshire, the author profited greatly from many stimulating discussions of teacher education with Dr. Butterfield. He has rendered the author a service in numerous consultations while the study was in progress. To him the author expresses gratitude.

The author has enlarged his own thinking in the philosophy of education in a year course and a summer session under Professor William H. Kilpatrick, to whom he is indebted.

The author was successively superintendent of schools, and deputy state superintendent of public instruction and director of educational research in the state department of education in New Hampshire during the period in which Dr. Henry C. Morrison, now professor of education in the University of Chicago, was state superintendent of public instruction. By constant and close association with him for a period of nine years in New Hampshire during part of the period with which this study deals, the author gained an understanding of Dr. Morrison's viewpoint in education and his philosophy of teacher education without which this dissertation could not have been written. To Dr. Morrison the author is deeply indebted, and to him he expresses appreciation for encouragement and inspiration.

Appreciation is expressed to Professor John K. Norton, who served on the author's dissertation committee.

HARRY A. BROWN

CONTENTS

PART I. THE PROBLEM AND THE METHOD

CHAPTER   PAGE

I. The Problem and the Method of Investigation   3

PART II. EARLY DEVELOPMENTS IN TEACHER EDU-
CATION UNDER DECENTRALIZATION

II. Beginnings in Teacher Education   15

III. Early Goals and Practices in Teacher Education   30

PART III. REORGANIZATION AND PROGRESS IN
TEACHER EDUCATION UNDER INCREASING
CENTRALIZATION

IV. Adoption of a State-wide Policy and Program of
Teacher Education   49

V. Reorganization and Extension of the Program for
the Education of Elementary-School Teachers   61

VI. Beginnings in the Establishment of Policies for the
Education and Professional Preparation of Secondary-School Teachers   76

VII. Progress in the Preparation of Secondary-School
Teachers   89

PART IV. BASIC POLICIES AND PRACTICES IN
TEACHER EDUCATION IN NEW HAMPSHIRE

VIII. The Struggle for Unity in the Public School System
Through the Establishment of Teachers Colleges   103

IX. Subject Matter in the Preparation of Elementary-
and Secondary-School Teachers   119

X. Development of Adequate Laboratory Schools   130

v

CHAPTER   PAGE

PART V. ACCOMPLISHMENTS IN TEACHER EDUCA-
TION UNDER A HIGH DEGREE OF
CENTRALIZATION

XI. PROGRESS TOWARD REALIZATION OF GOALS OF TEACHER
EDUCATION   141

XII. A UNIFIED STATE PROGRAM OF EDUCATION AND CERTIFI-
CATION OF TEACHERS   152

XIII. PRESENT VALUES IN TEACHER EDUCATION IN NEW HAMP-
SHIRE   165

BIBLIOGRAPHY   181

PART I

THE PROBLEM AND THE METHOD

CHAPTER I

THE PROBLEM AND THE METHOD OF
INVESTIGATION

INTRODUCTION

IN RECENT years several studies of teacher-education institutions
have been made with special reference to their organization, control,
and administration. These investigations have revealed significant facts concerning both internal and external control of teachers
colleges and normal schools. The forms of administrative control by
boards of different types which exist throughout the United States
are now understood in considerable detail.[1] The forms of legislative
control have been investigated and the types of legal control which
have been established are known.[2] The data in this field are now
somewhat out of date, for this study was made a decade and a half
ago and many changes have occurred since that time. More recently internal administration of teachers colleges through faculty
committees has been studied and important facts have been discovered.[3] Still more recently other features of the internal administration of teachers colleges have been the subject of investigations.
The latest study contained significant recommendations for internal
organization and administration of these institutions.[4] An early
study of teacher education in a single state urged simplification and
centralization of state educational organization in the interests of
better education of teachers.[5]

[1] Street, Claude A. *State Control of Teacher Training in the United States.*
Pittsburg, Kansas: Kansas State Teachers College. 1932.

[2] Hill, Lawrence B. *The Legislative Control of State Normal Schools.* New
York: Bureau of Publications, Teachers College, Columbia University. 1921.

[3] Sherrod, Charles C. *The Administration of State Teachers Colleges Through
Faculty Committees.* Nashville, Tennessee: George Peabody College for Teachers.
1925.

[4] Morrison, Robert H. *Internal Administrative Organization in Teachers Colleges.* New York: Bureau of Publications, Teachers College, Columbia University.
1933.

[5] Learned, William S., Bagley, William C., and Others. "Reorganization of State
Educational Control." *The Professional Preparation of Teachers for American
Public Schools,* p. 63. 1920.

3

These studies have provided valuable data concerning the organization and control of institutions for the preparation of teachers. They also contain recommendations for improvement in control, organization, and administration.

PRELIMINARY STATEMENT OF THE PURPOSE OF THE INVESTIGATION

The purpose of the present study is to investigate teacher-education procedures and their results in a single state during a particular period in which certain fundamental policies and programs of considerable significance were brought to fruition and yielded results which add materially to the understanding and insight needed as an aid in shaping new ends and purposes and establishing new procedures in teacher education. A preliminary survey of the states was made to determine those in which in recent years there have been carried on constructive developments which seemed worthy of special study and likely to yield significant findings. A dozen states were briefly studied to find one in which it seemed likely that important innovations have occurred representing changes which have significance and value as aids in further development of teacher education at the present time. The attempt was made to select a state in which the findings of a historical study would have a significant application and pertinence to present-day conditions.

MORE SPECIFIC PURPOSE OF THE STUDY

The state of New Hampshire was chosen for the investigation. Several reasons favored the choice of that state for the study. For approximately a quarter of a century the control and administration of state normal schools were directly in the hands of the state department of education and especially great efforts were devoted to the development of those schools as a part of a unified program of education in the state. The plan of organization for the administration of normal schools is a clearly defined type. The development of the New Hampshire school system has been investigated, and full information is available concerning the administration and control of education in that state. Data are available in state reports and other documents with which to determine what policies and procedures in teacher education have prevailed in New Hampshire. It is possible from the records to determine with considerable accuracy what results have been obtained. It seems clear that highly significant programs and policies of teacher education have been developed in New Hampshire.

More specifically, the purpose of this study is: (*a*) to describe in some detail the plan of state educational organization which exists in New Hampshire for the control of teacher education; (*b*) to show how this plan has evolved and what influences and forces were responsible for the development which took place; (*c*) to determine what policies and procedures in teacher education have been dominant in the state at different periods; and (*d*) to discover what significant results have come from these policies and their fulfillment which contribute values useful in finding better ways to conduct the enterprise of teacher education.

TYPES OF STATE CONTROL OF TEACHER EDUCATION

Five types of state control of teacher education are found in the United States. They have been described as follows:

I. The type in which each of several state institutions engaged in the professional preparation of teachers is under the major control of its own separate board of trustees.

II. The type in which the several state institutions devoted exclusively to the professional preparation of teachers are under the control of a single board which does not have jurisdiction over the public school system or other state institutions of higher learning.

III. The type in which all state institutions engaged in the professional preparation of teachers are under the major control of a board of higher education which does not have jurisdiction over the public school system.

IV. The type in which all state institutions devoted exclusively to the professional preparation of teachers are under the major control of a state board or department of education, which has jurisdiction over the public school system, but does not control other state institutions of higher learning.

V. The type in which all state institutions devoted exclusively to the professional preparation of teachers are under the control of a state board of education which has jurisdiction over the public school system and also controls other state institutions of higher learning.[6]

TYPE OF CONTROL OF TEACHER EDUCATION
IN NEW HAMPSHIRE

Public education in New Hampshire is under the jurisdiction of a state board of education appointed by the governor for terms of five years. The board is composed of seven members. Two members must be chosen from the personnel of the board of trustees of the state university. The state board of education appoints a com-

[6] Street. *Op. cit.*, p. 2.

missioner of education who is the secretary and executive officer of the board. The state normal schools are under the complete jurisdiction of the state board of education, which administers them through the commissioner of education. The actual management is delegated to the presidents who communicate with the board through the commissioner. Policies, programs, budgets, and similar problems are decided by the board, under the advisement of the commissioner. The presidents confer with the commissioner concerning policies, and recommendations go to the board from the commissioner. In a word, the board, with the advice of the commissioner, approves teacher-education policies, which are then executed by the commissioner but largely through direct action of the presidents. New Hampshire has a separate board of trustees for the state university. This form of administration of teacher-education institutions clearly conforms to the fourth type under the classifications previously described.

HIGHLY CENTRALIZED TYPE OF EDUCATIONAL ADMINISTRATION IN NEW HAMPSHIRE

It is said that no more highly centralized form of state educational control and administration exists in the United States than that found in New Hampshire. After an extended study of the development of the state school system in New Hampshire and a consideration of its present status, Bishop concluded:

Evidence would seem to show that no state in the Union has, at the present time, a higher degree of centralization of authority and power in the organization, administration, and support of the public schools than has New Hampshire. In no state does the law, in general, give greater power to a state-wide authority to initiate, direct, and decide the educational policy and practice which is to affect each of the small local communities. And it might also be said that there is no better example of the effects upon educational attainment of different degrees of centralization and decentralization of authority in the organization and administration of the common public schools than that which is to be found in the educational history of the state of New Hampshire.[7]

STATUTES GOVERNING STATE EDUCATIONAL ORGANIZATION

The statute under which the present state board of education was organized was enacted in 1919 and contained this provision:

[7] Bishop, Eugene A. *The Development of a State School System: New Hampshire*, p. 2. New York: Bureau of Publications, Teachers College, Columbia University. 1930.

A board to be designated as the State Board of Education, consisting of five members, in addition to the governor, as member *ex-officio*, is hereby created. The members, not more than three of whom shall belong to the same political party, shall not be technical educators nor professionally engaged in school work, but public-spirited and interested citizens willing to serve the state without pay and to give the time necessary for an understanding of the educational needs of the state, and of the best way to apply them.[8]

The provision that the board should be enlarged to seven members, two of whom are required to be members of the board of trustees of the University of New Hampshire, was added in a later amendment. The reference to political parties was omitted in the revision.

The legislature which enacted the new education law of 1919 provided for a high degree of centralization of power by decreeing that:

The state board shall have the same powers of management, supervision and direction over all public schools in this state as the directors of the ordinary business corporation have over the business of the corporation, except as its powers and duties may be limited by law. It may make all rules and regulations necessary for the management of its own business and for the conduct of its officers, employees and agents, and further may make such rules and regulations as may seem desirable to secure the efficient administration of the public schools . . . and it shall be the duty of school boards and employees of school districts to comply with the rules and regulations of the state board.[9]

CONTROL OF NORMAL SCHOOLS BY STATE BOARD OF EDUCATION

The control and management of the state normal schools, which had formerly resided in a board of trustees, was given to the new state board of education in the education law of 1919. Under the statute, in which the board was given an extensive general grant of authority over the entire public school system of the state, the state normal schools were included as an essential part of the system of public education. The transfer of normal schools to the state board of education was accomplished in the following stipulation:

The state board shall exercise the powers and perform the duties now exercised and performed by the superintendent of public instruction, the trustees of the state normal schools, the state board for vocational education, and shall take over the business of the above-named officers and boards. . . .[10]

[8] *Laws of New Hampshire Relating to Public Schools.* Session Laws of 1919. Chapter 106.
[9] *Ibid.*
[10] *Ibid.*

The law provided for a qualified administrative officer in the following provision:

> The state board shall employ a skilled executive officer who shall have had training and experience in educational work. Such person shall be the chief executive officer of said board and shall be its secretary, and shall be called the commissioner of education. Said commissioner shall be appointed for an indefinite term and shall be subject to removal upon the majority vote of the entire board, and said board shall fix his salary and prescribe his duties except as the same may be prescribed by law. Said commissioner need not be a resident of the state at the time of his appointment.[11]

These and other sections of the statute which was enacted into law in 1919 as the basis for a drastic reorganization of the educational system of the state brought to a climax a tendency toward centralization which had been in progress for more than three decades. The New Hampshire system of public education began in 1846 as a highly decentralized system and progressed by slow steps to its present form. The new education law was somewhat revised in 1921 but its essential features were retained. Since the progress from decentralization to centralization has been investigated and described, that aspect of educational development in New Hampshire forms no part of this study except that it is later briefly reviewed.

PRECISE DEFINITION AND LIMITATION OF THE PROBLEM

As this study progressed, it seemed desirable to limit it to certain questions of significance for teacher education in general. Many subjects of importance had to be omitted. The study is limited to teacher education as conducted in the state normal schools. The questions of financing teacher education, levels of preparation in the teaching staff of the state, in-service education of teachers, teacher supply and demand, and the theory of higher education with reference to teacher education which prevailed and many other similar problems had to be omitted. The course of development in these particulars was not sufficiently different from that in other states to warrant their inclusion. Those problems, however, were all considered. The criterion by which it was decided to omit or include historical and interpretative study of any aspect of teacher education in New Hampshire was the question: What programs, policies, trends, forces, movements, and causes in teacher educa-

[11] *Laws of New Hampshire Relating to Public Schools.* Session Laws of 1919. Chapter 106.

tion, operating in New Hampshire, when historically studied and interpreted, contribute significantly to the understanding and insight needed as the basis for intelligent action in the present and future in the preparation of teachers in the United States? The questions studied follow:

1. What was the character of the beginnings in teacher education in the state? What impulses and purposes dominated? To what ends were they directed? What theories or practices which may aid in solving present-day teacher-education problems came from them?

2. What was the nature of the processes of evolution of teacher-education policies and practices in earlier and later periods? To what ends did evolution move?

3. What radical readjustments or comprehensive developments of a revolutionary character occurred? What were their effects? What innovations were established which demonstrated fundamental principles of teacher education? What trends were set in motion which represented valuable contributions to the theory and practice of teacher education?

4. What difficulties were encountered? How were they met? Were they overcome? What lessons may be learned from these experiences?

5. What problems needing solution existed during the period under consideration? In what manner were they attacked? How were they solved? What light is shed on present problems of teacher education by the modes of attack which were used at that time and the solutions which were attained?

6. What failures occurred? What caused the failures? What procedures would have prevented the failure?

7. What philosophies of teacher education containing essential truth were enunciated? What curriculum principles were developed?

8. What programs of teacher education finally were developed?

9. How did the final type of control of teacher education originate? How did it develop into the centralized type of administration which now exists in New Hampshire?

10. What values are found in the course of historical development and the present status of teacher education in New Hampshire?

LIMITATIONS OF THE STUDY

This investigation is limited to a single state. It is further restricted to discovering what happened in certain aspects of teacher education and to interpreting the significance of what was found. The study is historical and interpretative and not statistical. An attempt will be made, however, to find causal relationships and to discover the forces and influences which accounted for what happened in teacher education.

METHOD OF INVESTIGATION

The method upon which chief reliance has been placed in this investigation was documentary study. The biennial reports of the state superintendent of public instruction and the reports of the state board of education were important sources of information. The catalogs of the two state normal schools from their establishment to the present time supplied many important facts. The laws of New Hampshire contained all of the enactments of the legislature with reference to teacher education. Numerous unpublished official reports on file in the office of the state board of education contained material which threw a good deal of light on the development of teacher education in the state and the policies underlying the programs and procedures which prevailed. Correspondence in the files of the state superintendent of public instruction and the commissioner of education contained significant material. Rules and regulations adopted by the state board of education, especially the regulations concerning the certification of teachers, were documents of especial importance. Proceedings of the state board of education, reports of the former trustees of the state normal schools and their proceedings, and the reports of the presidents of the normal schools to the commissioner of education were especially significant sources from which data were obtained. Several histories of education in New Hampshire contributed much valuable information.

Particular sources of the most significant information were: (a) chapters dealing with the preparation of teachers in the earlier reports of the state superintendent of public instruction and later the commissioner of education of New Hampshire, in which programs and policies under consideration were discussed; (b) the reports of the commissioner of education during the past decade, which contain a good deal of factual material concerning the progress of teacher education in the state and the results accomplished in successive bienniums; (c) records on file in the state education office at Concord, which contain valuable unpublished material.

It was necessary to read all the state education reports from 1846 to 1934, to scan the statutes of the state with reference to particular enactments, to read portions of several histories of the state, to study all the catalogs of the normal schools since the establishment of the first school in 1871, to read much material in the files of the state board of education, to correspond and confer with the present and the former commissioner of education and the former state superintendent of public instruction, to study many publications of the state board of education and to discuss various problems personally with the two presidents.

PART II

EARLY DEVELOPMENTS IN TEACHER EDUCATION UNDER DECENTRALIZATION

CHAPTER II

BEGINNINGS IN TEACHER EDUCATION

SOME EARLY HISTORY

THE earliest history of New Hampshire has little to say about education. The people who established the first settlements in 1623 and 1638 provided their own schools. Each settlement was independent of the others. No state-wide educational control existed. Teachers had no professional preparation. The first education law enacted by the colony of Massachusetts merely required parents to give instruction to their children. In 1647 a law was passed establishing elementary schools in the colony. This happened before New Hampshire became a separate state. Twenty years later each town was required to have a building and to furnish a teacher.[1]

After New Hampshire separated from Massachusetts in 1650 a period of eighty-four years elapsed with no educational legislation of any consequence except that which re-enacted early Massachusetts laws as statutes of the state of New Hampshire. Only minor changes were made in these laws. It is probable that in that early period schools were not effective in any real sense. The constitution of the state, adopted in 1783, made a strong pronouncement concerning education. A new school law was passed in 1789 which provided for levying a tax for schools, authorized examinations for teachers by supposedly competent local authorities—a minister or some other educated person—and made compulsory the teaching of reading, writing, and arithmetic. After the Revolutionary War the state developed rapidly and interest in education grew at the same time. The education law of 1827 established town school committees and took the management of schools away from the selectmen under whom education had been considerably retarded. This committee, it was said, was required to visit and inspect schools, to examine and certify teachers, to select textbooks, and to make to the town an annual report upon the condition of the schools.[2] Each

[1] Butterfield, E. W. "History of New Hampshire Schools and School Legislation." *Report of the State Board of Education*, p. 47. 1924.
[2] *Ibid.*, p. 47.

district within each town had a prudential committee which employed teachers and in other details managed the schools. The school district law passed in 1805 had permitted the creation of many small school districts in each town, and each was an independent unit for school purposes. This represented local control of schools carried to an extreme. It resulted in great inefficiency. Up to this time no provision had been made by the state for the preparation of teachers.

FIRST TEACHER EDUCATION LAW

It was in 1846 that the first law was enacted which made any provision for the professional education of teachers in the state. That statute established the office of state commissioner of common schools. It also provided for teachers' institutes for the preparation of teachers for common schools, which in those days meant chiefly the one-teacher district schools. The law authorized the towns to make a small annual appropriation for an institute to be held within the county. In 1867 a fund, derived from the sale of state lands, was created for the support of institutes.

EARLY FORMS OF STATE EDUCATIONAL ORGANIZATION

That first form of state school organization established in 1846 was soon changed. In 1850 the statutes authorized the position of county school commissioner in each county. The county commissioners constituted a state board of education. They elected one of their number secretary of the board. With three exceptions the secretaries were changed every year until 1867 when the board was abolished. From 1868 to 1873 New Hampshire had a state board of education which consisted of the governor and his council. During this period it also had a state superintendent of public instruction who was appointed by the governor and council. Beginning with 1874, however, the governor and council no longer served as a board. The office of state superintendent of public instruction was continued until the passage of the new education law in 1919 which, as has already been pointed out, again provided for a state board of education with a commissioner of education as its executive officer.

It is convenient for the purposes of this study to divide the history of education in New Hampshire into three periods so far as teacher education is concerned. (a) The first period includes the years in which educational affairs in the state were administered successively by the state commissioners of common schools, the county commissioners of common schools serving as a state board of education, and the first three state superintendents of public instruction. This period extends from 1846 to 1904, the date of the beginning of the administration of Henry C. Morrison as state superintendent. (b) The second period extends from 1904 to 1919 and includes Morrison's administration as state superintendent of public instruction and that of Ernest W. Butterfield in the same office. (c) The third period is that of the state board of education created in 1919 and includes the years of Butterfield's administration as commissioner of education and those of James N. Pringle, the present commissioner.

DECENTRALIZATION DURING THE EARLY PERIOD

During the first period decentralization of a rather extreme sort characterized state school administration in New Hampshire. None of the early state commissioners of common schools continued in office for any extended period. They had little authority and devoted only a part of their time to the office to which they had been appointed. In the period of the county commissioners a new board and a new secretary of the board came upon the scene every twelve months. When the governor and his council served as the state board of education, they had little control over education except to appoint a state superintendent of public instruction. He in turn had little statutory authority. He was required to give lectures throughout the state, to hold teachers' insitutes, and to write a report. Even during the early years of Morrison's administration he had little power except that which came from his personal leadership.

PERIOD OF DISTRICT DOMINATION

The earliest period has been characterized as the period of district domination.[3] The law permitting the abolition of the school districts in any town was passed in 1870 and districts were finally prohibited in 1892.[4] However, the dominating characteristic of this period, namely, that of decentralization in educational administration, extended beyond that date. The state office of education continued to have little authority and the towns and cities were largely independent of any state control or administration in the management of their schools.

[3] Bishop. *Op. cit.*, p. 33.　　　　[4] Bishop. *Op. cit.*, pp. 71-72.

TEACHERS' INSTITUTES AND STATE NORMAL SCHOOL

Two facts in this early period are of especially great interest. The first is the popularity of the teachers' institutes as a factor in teacher education. The second is the rise and development of the normal school idea in New Hampshire. Teachers' institutes are not given special treatment in this study. The remainder of this chapter is devoted to the campaign for the establishment of a state normal school and to a discussion of the organization of the first state normal school in the state.

CONCEPTION OF GOOD SCHOOLS AS THE STATE'S SAFEGUARD

The idea that an illiterate community is a danger to the state runs all through the discussions in the early reports of the commissioners of common schools. Good schools were everywhere indicated as the means by which the common enlightenment and the generally informed intelligence, believed to be the safeguard of the state, may be attained. Again and again references were made to the need for good teachers in the common schools. The idea was continuously stressed that the quality of citizenship of the state depends upon the quality of the public schools. The zeal of the crusader, in the interests of better teachers and improved schools, breathes from the pages of those early reports. Commissioner Rust said, in 1849, that the safety of the state depends upon the education of every child. He declared that every ignorant and corrupt person is a danger to the prosperity, morals, and happiness of the entire state.[5] On another occasion, he declared:

The elementary education of our youth is essential to civilized society and the perpetuating of our free institutions, and therefore, should be secured at whatever expense may be necessary. Such has been the opinion of the fathers. Education is of such paramount importance and so intimately connected with our political existence that a tax has been levied upon the property of the state for the instruction of its youth. Our system of Common Schools is based on the principle that the property of the several towns must educate their children, and a similar one is involved in all cases, where private benefit is secured by advancing the general good. It is universally admitted that none but intelligent people can be permanently free and happy. Self-preservation, therefore, impels the state to the education of its youth.[6]

[5] Rust, Richard S. *Third Annual Report of the Commissioner of Common Schools*, p. 27. 1850.
[6] *Ibid.*, p. 50.

Similar quotations in great numbers could be made from the reports of the early commissioners and state superintendents, indicating such a conception of the place and value of public education. It is easy to see why the need for the best possible preparation of teachers received so much emphasis at this time.

EARLY TEACHER QUALIFICATIONS

In this early period no qualifications were required of teachers of the common schools except that they be examined by the superintending school committee of the town. After such examination it was legal for the prudential committee of any school district in the town to employ a teacher so certificated. No other standards of certification were required.[7] It was impossible, of course, to maintain a well-qualified teaching staff under such requirements. There is no evidence to indicate that teachers had more than a meager common-school education except in the case of those young men who taught winter terms and those who had some preparation in the academies. The number in each of these groups cannot be determined, but it could not have been large.

Teaching was not looked upon as a profession which offered opportunities to promising young men and women. Commissioner Rust accurately described the few opportunities open to young people in teaching when he stated that:

The compensation and reputation connected with what are termed the learned professions are strong incitements to effort in aspiring candidates, while a situation in the district school has associated with it none of these motives. The charms of the school are few and dim in the estimation of the talented son of genius, and he prefers any other road to fame and wealth, rather than that of teaching.[8]

While the district school teachers of those days possessed in general the most meager academic background for their work and had practically no professional preparation, even as understood at that time, some evidence exists that they were an aspiring and earnest group of people. It was a primitive period with schools and teachers who matched the crude and simple characteristics of the age. Methods of teaching in the common schools were not founded upon any philosophy of education at all comparable to present-day conceptions; they consisted of little but drill and memorization. The

[7] *Ibid.*, p. 45.
[8] *Ibid.*, p. 45.

need of better-prepared teachers, however, was keenly realized by many leaders in education and by many citizens who were prominent in the public life of the state. In fact one of the most encouraging facts about the whole situation is this realization of the inadequacy of the schools and the insufficient preparation of teachers. Many of the leaders of that day manifestly understood the function of education in a civilized society. They had high aspirations toward better preparation of teachers as the means of attaining a stable and progressive society which, through the processes of education acting within the society, might make possible social evolution toward a better state of human relations.

EARLY REFERENCE TO THE NORMAL-SCHOOL IDEA

The idea of a state normal school was clearly in the minds of the early state commissioners of common schools. References to such an institution are found as early as the second report of the commissioner, which was presented to the June session of the legislature in 1848. In that report the commissioner said that:

The establishment of a permanent normal school is so expensive and would be attended with so much embarrassment, that the agitation of the question, at the present time, is not deemed desirable. Yet we trust that the time is not far distant when a teachers' seminary shall be established which shall be an honor and a blessing to the state.[9]

After the second report of the commissioner of common schools references to the need for a state normal school are found in nearly every report. At first the desirability of such a school was affirmed, but a doubt of the possibility or wisdom of establishing such an institution was either expressed or clearly implied. At a later date, after the first state board of education was established, J. W. Patterson, its secretary, comparing the value of teachers' institutes and normal schools wrote:

If we can have but one, and it is possible to bring about a general attendance of teachers—which we doubt—I should not hesitate to give the preference to the thorough drill, the professional training and enthusiasm of the normal school. . . . If the Law and Divinity can rightfully demand special schools for their disciples, then Teaching can lay a higher claim upon the community for professional schools, because hitherto more neglected than they.[10]

Referring to objections currently made to institutes in which it was

[9] Rust, Richard S. *Report of the Commissioner of Common Schools*, p. 37. 1848.
[10] Patterson, J. W. *Twelfth Annual Report upon the Common Schools of New Hampshire*, p. 20. 1858.

asserted that it was necessary for the different instructors to give lectures rather than to drill their classes in the subjects taught, Patterson continued by saying:

The objection to which we have referred has great weight as an argument in favor of normal schools, and we trust the people and the legislature will feel its force, and be led, at no distant day, to establish one or more institutions, of this nature, such as the welfare and position of the state demand.[11]

By the time the ninth annual report of the board of education was issued in June, 1855, a good deal of the doubt about the possibility of establishing a state normal school had disappeared. Only traces of it remained. Secretary King S. Hall of the board of education said that year in his annual report that:

The friends of education have long regarded a state normal school as very desirable, yet have had doubts as to the practicability of its immediate establishment. These doubts are being removed; and from various quarters the subject has been strongly advocated.[12]

During that year the state teachers association adopted a resolution advocating the establishment of a state normal school. Moreover it agreed to pay $2,500 a year toward the salaries of the faculty provided that the legislature would appropriate a similar amount for that purpose.[13] Secretary Hall was emphatic in his statement that the time had come when the preliminary steps should be taken to found a state normal school.

In 1863 John Wingate, Jr., made an extended plea for the establishment of a state normal school and based his argument on the fact that a "school system can never be complete without a thorough method of educating teachers."[14]

Frequently in the earliest reports an optimistic tone concerning the excellence of the schools was evident, but later this note disappeared and the defects of the schools became more evident. Secretary Roger M. Sargent of the state board of education in 1864 concluded a discussion of the excellences and weaknesses of the schools with the statement that "Our system is partly successful and partly a failure."[15] Then he continued by discussing the lack of facilities

[11] *Ibid.*, p. 20.
[12] Hall, King S. "Facilities for the Improvement of Teachers." *Ninth Annual Report upon the Schools of New Hampshire*, p. 42. 1855. [13] *Ibid.*, p. 42.
[14] Wingate, Jr., John. *Seventeenth Annual Report upon the Common Schools of New Hampshire*, p. 14. 1863.
[15] Sargent, Roger M. *Eighteenth Annual Report upon the Common Schools of New Hampshire*, p. 9. 1864.

for preparing teachers. He assigned the lack of good teachers as the cause of the deficiencies in the schools of the state. Sargent continued the earnest pleas of his predecessors in the office of secretary of the board of education for better preparation of teachers. He said:

The greatest requisite for successful schools is competent teachers. At present there is a great deficiency of these. We have enough and to spare, who have been over a range of studies and offer themselves as teachers, but who have had no opportunity to learn the science of teaching, and no instruction in its art.[16]

The argument for a state normal school became more and more urgent each year and in 1866 Secretary George W. Cate went on record by saying that:

It is to the dishonor of our noble state that we have no school where students may receive instruction especially designed to prepare them for teaching. Normal schools have been established in other states, and have been successful. None can doubt their utility in our own, if rightly conducted. Our schools are suffering more today for want of live, experienced, and thorough teachers, than from any other one thing.[17]

More and more of the time of the meetings of the state board of education was devoted to discussion of the need for better teachers and the necessity for one or more state normal schools.[18]

The reader who follows through the reports of the commissioner of common schools and the state board of education during this period gets the strong feeling as he reads the reports after 1863 that the establishment of a state normal school was near at hand. The first state superintendent of public instruction in his first report made in June, 1868, deplored the abolition of teachers' institutes and declared that there existed "entire unanimity of sentiment in favor of the restoration of teachers' institutes and the establishment of the normal school in some form."[19] These institutes were re-established in 1868 and ten were held during the year ending in June, 1869, but this did not lessen the argument for a state normal school. In his report for 1869 Hadley devoted considerable space to the argument for a normal school and quoted Mann and Guyzot. His plea

[16] *Ibid.*, p. 9.

[17] Cate, George W. *Twentieth Annual Report upon the Common Schools of New Hampshire*, p. 7. 1866.

[18] Sargent, Roger M. "Meetings of the Board." *Twenty-first Annual Report upon the Common Schools of New Hampshire*, pp. 5-15. 1867.

[19] Hadley, Amos. *Annual Report of the Board of Education and Superintendent of Public Instruction*, p. 11. 1868.

for a normal school in that report was the strongest yet presented.[20] He called attention to the number of such schools in Great Britain, France, and Prussia, and recounted the success of the schools in those countries. He restated the fact that all of the newer states had established normal schools immediately upon their admission to the Union. He said that the South was accomplishing reconstruction in part through education and establishing normal schools to make public education effective. He stressed the fact that all the older states except Ohio and New Hampshire had established state normal schools. It was not a rhetorical question when Hadley asked:

Is it for the honor or the interest of New Hampshire to be thus an exception, with only one other state to keep her in countenance, and that one casting about to bring herself within the general rule of progress and join the company of the other sisters gone ahead?[21]

Hadley's concluding argument is so well expressed that the reader of his report of 1869, in which he seemed to put all the eloquence at his command into a plea for a normal school, confidently expects on turning to the next report to read the account of the establishment of such an institution. These are the words which Hadley used:

For surely none will deny that the state is bound to provide for the maintenance of the common school at the public expense, or that it is also bound to provide the means for best effectuating the purpose of such maintenance, which is the thorough elementary education of all its children. To effectuate best this purpose, the best teaching is requisite; and for procuring this, the experience of nearly two centuries and of two hemispheres has attested the best means to be professional training in the normal school.[22]

Public sentiment had so crystallized by this time and the demand for a normal school was so insistent from the pulpit, in educational associations, in teachers' institutes, and other popular assemblages that it seemed irresistible.[23]

EFFECTS OF THE MASSACHUSETTS CAMPAIGN IN NEW HAMPSHIRE

The evidence is clear that the campaign for the establishment of normal schools in Massachusetts was successfully carried over into

[20] Hadley, Amos. "The Normal School." *Annual Report of the Board of Education and Superintendent of Public Instruction*, pp. 25-38. 1869.
[21] *Ibid.*, p. 27.   [22] *Ibid.*, pp. 31-32.   [23] *Ibid.*, p. 33.

New Hampshire. It appears that Charles Brooks made three visits to New Hampshire—in 1837, in 1838, and in 1839. The opinion has been recorded that:

> . . . no individual in the whole country has done more to arouse the public mind of New England to the importance of normal schools, and to some extent, the leading minds of some other states, than the Rev. Charles Brooks. He lectured before the Legislature of New Hampshire by their request at Concord, on the 13th, 14th and 15th of June, 1837 and 1838, and again in 1845 and in the former year at Keene, Portsmouth, Concord and Nashua. . . .[24]

Brooks's visit to New Hampshire in the interest of normal schools was undoubtedly productive in adding materially to the interest which already existed. State Commissioner R. S. Rust, in his second annual report, quoted a letter from J. Prentiss of Cheshire County, which had been a pioneer in holding teachers' institutes. Prentiss's letter, under date of May 2, 1848, which came in reply, contained these words:

> The very able lectures of Rev. Charles Brooks in this county, about ten years ago (which were also given before the Legislature at Concord) contributed to give a new impulse. Mr. Brooks had traveled much in Europe and was thoroughly acquainted with the best systems of schools in Prussia, France and other countries. Normal schools were felt by many to be indispensable for improvement here; and attempts were made in 1839 and in subsequent years to obtain legislative aid and action but without success. . . . And now I am ready to answer one of your questions, so far as our experience has gone. County institutes may meet the wants of our state, for the preparation of teachers. Still, a State Technical Seminary is desirable, if only to raise up and qualify Principals and Assistants for our County Institutes. I do not think much of any provision in an Academy for a Teachers' Department.[25]

The campaign to establish a state normal school in New Hampshire was thus long and arduous. The period in which it was waged has been called that of the rise of the state normal schools.[26] The period of Pestalozzian influence,[27] which extended from 1860 to 1890, was well started before New Hampshire established a state normal school. The first twelve state normal schools organized in

[24] Barnard, Henry. *Normal Schools and Other Institutions, Agencies and Means Designed for the Professional Education of Teachers: Part I. United States and Provinces*, p. 157.

[25] Rust, Richard S. "Teachers' Institute" (Letter from John Prentiss quoted). *Report of the Commissioner of Common Schools*, pp. 40-41. 1848.

[26] Napier, Thomas H. *Trends in the Curricula for Training Teachers*, p. 44.

[27] *Ibid.*, p. 63.

this country were well established. Oswego was vigorously demonstrating Pestalozzianism. A training school was in operation at Oswego as a laboratory for the professional preparation of teachers with ample provision for observation, demonstration, and practice. At St. Cloud, Minnesota, Gray was developing his conception of a normal school as a technical school of university grade.[28] Other normal schools were flourishing at New Britain, Connecticut, at Albany, New York, at Ypsilanti, Michigan, at Normal, Illinois, and at several other places. Thus the normal-school movement was well established before New Hampshire finally took action. The state normal school at Plymouth was established in 1870 and began its first term March 15, 1871.

FIRST CURRICULUM AT PLYMOUTH

Two curricula were established at the founding of the state normal school at Plymouth. Each was one year in length. One was called the "First Course" and the other the "Second Course." A good deal of information concerning these curricula is available, for they were printed in all the early catalogs. They were also reproduced and discussed in the reports of the state superintendent of public instruction.

The first curricula are presented here as they appeared in 1873.[29] They are of great historical interest in showing one example of the form which the early curricula of the state normal school assumed in this country. They have a peculiar interest and significance for another reason which will be discussed at a later point. The following is the form of the "First Course" as published in the Plymouth catalog:

1. Arithmetic, Mental and Written
2. Geography, with Map Drawing
3. History of the United States
4. Constitution of the United States and of New Hampshire
5. English Grammar
6. Bookkeeping
7. Reading, including the Elements of Elocution and Vocal Culture
8. Spelling, including Derivation and Definition
9. Penmanship
10. Elements of Drawing, Botany and Physiology

It was provided also that students should have work in composition and declamation throughout the year. The early catalogs carried statements to the effect that members of the graduating class

[28] *Ibid.*, p. 75.
[29] *Catalog of the Officers and Students of the State Normal School at Plymouth, New Hampshire*, p. 18. 1873.

and students in the "Second Course" would have opportunities to take charge of classes in the model school, as the training school was then called. Other evidence, however, indicates that little or no student teaching was done at the beginning. Principal Horatio O. Ladd, in his report to the state board of education under date of April 28, 1874, stated concerning the model schools that:

These schools are now well graded and well taught. They afford no material benefit to the normal school, except still further to identify the interests of the citizens of Plymouth with its prosperity.[30]

It can be safely concluded that little or no student teaching was done at that date. The principal recorded the fact that he taught all the advanced studies in the "Second Course" and also three or four of the "First Course," and at the same time attended to all the administration. This required, he said, seven or eight hours a day in the classroom.[31] One assistant teacher, two student assistants, and two teachers in the model school constituted the faculty for 122 normal-school students and 142 pupils in the model school. No effective supervision of student teaching could have been done.

The "Second Course," as published in the catalog of 1873, was said to consist of the higher English branches.[32] It required no foreign language and was devoted largely to English, mathematics, and elementary short courses in natural sciences. The curriculum follows:

1. Algebra
2. Physical Geography
3. Physiology'
4. Botany
5. Natural Philosophy
6. Bookkeeping
7. Drawing
8. Rhetoric, including Critical Expositions of Standard Authors in Prose and Poetry
9. Two of the following: Geology, Intellectual Philosophy, Moral Philosophy, Political Economy, Evidences of Christianity

As in the "First Course," work in composition and declamation was required throughout the year.

ADMISSION REQUIREMENTS

For admission to the "First Course" students were required to pass a satisfactory examination in arithmetic, upon the fundamental

---

[30] Ladd, Horatio O. "Report of State Normal School." *Annual Report of the Board of Education and Superintendent of Public Instruction*, p. 15. 1874.

[31] *Ibid.*, p. 12.

[32] *Catalog of the Officers and Students of the State Normal School at Plymouth, New Hampshire*, pp. 18-19. 1873.

rules as applied to simple and compound numbers and fractions, both common and decimal; in geography, upon the natural divisions of land and water, the political divisions of the earth, and the general geography of New Hampshire; in grammar, upon grammatical definitions and inflections, with parsing and the analysis of sentences.[33] It was provided also that holders of institute certificates might be admitted without examination. These certificates were based upon attendance at several sessions of the teachers' institutes of the state. It is clear that the admission requirements included only the most rudimentary knowledge of three of the common-school studies of that day.

PREPARATORY CURRICULUM

Shortly after the establishment of the school it was found that a preparatory curriculum seemed desirable to "furnish practical knowledge to students not sufficiently informed to receive training as teachers."[34] This curriculum was of the most elementary character and made possible entrance to the normal school for those with even more rudimentary education than the first entrance requirements contemplated. This preparatory curriculum covered the following studies:

Arithmetic—Elementary, Practical to Interest
Geography—to Africa, with Map Drawing
English Grammar—Language Lessons and Parsing
Reading, Spelling, and Penmanship
Elements of Drawing

The "First Course" began where the preparatory curriculum ended. It was recorded that in the "First Course" arithmetic, for example, began with interest, geography with Africa. This curriculum is presented to show the very elementary nature of the earliest normal school curriculum in New Hampshire. Apparently the simplest literacy was the only condition of admission. Rudimentary proficiency in the common branches, with some notion of how to teach these subjects in the common school, was the objective of the "First Course," which included the majority of students during the first decade and a half of the history of the school.

[33] *Catalog of the Officers and Students of the State Normal School at Plymouth, New Hampshire*, p. 17. 1873. This paragraph is reproduced almost verbatim from the catalog.
[34] *Fourth Annual Catalog of the Officers and Students of the New Hampshire State Normal School*, p. 18. 1873-1874.

PURPOSES OF THE NORMAL SCHOOL

Clear evidence is presented in the act which provided for the establishment of the normal school that both courses of study contemplated preparation of teachers for only the common schools, which in those days were considered to be the district ungraded schools and the graded elementary schools in the larger towns and cities. Section 7 of the act makes the certificate of graduation from the lower course (one year) a license to teach in the common schools of the state for three years, and from the higher course a license to teach in those schools for five years.[35]

Further evidence that the purpose of the institution was the preparation of teachers for the ungraded district schools of the state is found in the report of the trustees presented in June, 1883. The board pointed out in this report that in earlier years pupils attended the district school until they were adults, but that at the later period of which they were writing children attended only until they were fifteen, and after that irregularly or not at all.[36] The district schools were in reality primary schools.[37] It seemed to the trustees that in view of these facts the curriculum should deal only with the elements of the common school studies. They said:

In furtherance of this plan the board lengthened the school year from 30 to 40 weeks; . . . limited instruction to the branches taught in a full ungraded school, and established a school of practice in which each candidate for a diploma must teach children 20 weeks under the eye of a critic teacher.[38]

A simple examination based upon the common school studies continued to be the condition of admission. In 1890-1891, twenty years after the founding of the school, this statement appeared in the catalog:

Candidates . . . must show upon examination good capacity and general intelligence, fair attainments in arithmetic, geography, and the English language (including reading, writing, spelling, grammar and composition) . . . but preparation for admission can be secured by the faithful student in the common schools.[39]

[35] "Laws Relating to the State Normal School, Section 7." *Seventh Annual Report of the Trustees of the State Normal School*, pp. 34-40.

[36] "Report of the Trustees." *Annual Report of the State Normal School of New Hampshire*, pp. 4-6. 1883.

[37] *Ibid.*, p. 4.

[38] *Ibid.*, p. 4.

[39] "Condition of Admission." *Twenty-second Annual Catalog and Circular of the State Normal School*, p. 59. 1892.

More and more high-school graduates and experienced teachers, however, were coming to the school and in 1903 high-school graduation was made the requirement for admission.

EARLY NORMAL SCHOOL RELATED ONLY TO THE COMMON SCHOOLS

In the early period in New Hampshire, a dual school system existed. The public high school had hardly come into existence. The academy was the main agency for secondary education. More than eighty academies existed at one time. They were private institutions and were not under public control; the commissioner of education had no jurisdiction over them. The system of education was not at that time divided in the complete double-track sense, as in Europe. There was one difference. In Europe the common school was a terminal school. This was not true in New Hampshire where pupils went from the district schools into the academies, in which some prepared to be teachers and returned to the district schools. The academies nevertheless devoted themselves largely to college preparation.

Thus the academies and the colleges were a school system set apart in large measure. The common schools and the normal school were to a considerable degree another school system. Students who came directly from the common schools to the normal school could not go on to college on the basis of their normal-school work. Neither did these normal-school studies parallel the work of the academies. Normal-school graduates were not prepared to teach in the academies. Thus at that time the New Hampshire normal school was a terminal school. It led only back into teaching in the district schools. It was thus in conception the German *Lehrerseminar*.

These facts are clear in the conception of the school which is evident in the state reports of that day. Thus the beginning of the New Hampshire normal school is one of the very good examples in this country of the projection of the German normal school for teachers of the common schools. It exemplified that idea in detail in its conception of the work and function of such an institution.

The manner in which this Prussian-conceived normal school of 1871, merely an upward extension of the elementary school with some pedagogical instruction, became the teachers college of 1934 with four-year post-secondary curricula, the right to grant a professional degree in education, and the privilege of preparing teachers for secondary as well as elementary schools, is a significant part of the history of teacher education in this country.

CHAPTER III

EARLY GOALS AND PRACTICES IN TEACHER EDUCATION

EARLY CURRICULUM CHANGES

CHANGES came slowly in the teacher-education curriculum at the state normal school at Plymouth. The first curriculum continued without material change during the first decade in the history of the institution; in fact, the only change of any consequence occurred in 1874 when student teaching was introduced. This consisted of teaching a class in the training school for a short period of time.

A new curriculum was established in 1882. The old idea of a "First Course" and a "Second Course" was abandoned in favor of a single continuous two-year curriculum. The preparatory curriculum was abandoned at that time and students entered directly upon the work of the first year.

A SIGNIFICANT INNOVATION IN TEACHER EDUCATION

An innovation was introduced in the curriculum of 1882 which represented at that time a revolutionary change in teacher education. With this new curriculum full-time, all-day student teaching was introduced. It is somewhat surprising to find such a conception of teacher education prevailing at so early a period. This was sixteen years after the state normal school at Oswego became a state institution. That institution had emphasized the work of the training school from the beginning and even before when it was a training school for the city teachers of Oswego. It is said that the class at Oswego was divided into two sections, each of which worked in the training school daily for an entire forenoon or an entire afternoon.[1] This practice at Plymouth by which all-day student teaching was introduced is believed to be the first instance in this country in which that was done. This antedated Burk's innovation in this particular by more than a decade and a half. With lapses at times this principle has continued to operate in New Hampshire normal schools

[1] Napier, Thomas H. *Trends in the Curricula for Training Teachers*, p. 67.

down to the present time. In 1882 the two years were divided into four twenty-week terms. Student teaching occurred in the fourth term; concerning it the catalog said:

Daily Work in the Training School: The training school corresponds to the five lower grades in a city school. The children are carefully graded, and assigned to the pupil [student] teachers in groups of ten. Each teacher has charge of the instruction and discipline of her class for ten weeks. She is then transferred to another class, and so has experience in teaching two grades. The pupil [student] teachers have one-half day each week for the inspection of work in the training school. Each evening [late afternoon, probably] Miss Reed [the critic teacher] meets the pupil teachers and discusses with them the work of the day: the work of the following day is assigned, and so for the term. Thus the theory and practice of teaching and school discipline are studied practically.

Special lessons in the elements of psychology are given by Miss Reed.[2]

The training school enrolled 100 children at that time. Eighteen student teachers were registered in the fourth term. This made available ten practice classes of ten pupils each, which permitted more than a half-day of continuous teaching for twenty weeks on the part of student teachers.

The new curriculum established in 1882-1883 consisted of three terms devoted largely to academic study, but it also included considerable pedagogical instruction.[3] The curriculum follows.

FIRST YEAR

First Term		Second Term	
Geometry	English	Geography	English
Geology	Music	History	Physiology
History	Drawing	Commercial arithmetic	

SECOND YEAR

Algebra	Daily teaching in the training
Physics	school; conferences with the critic
English	teacher; theory and practice of
Elementary arithmetic	teaching studied practically; psy-
Elements of mental science	chology studied in connection.

A recent experiment in teacher education which has attracted wide attention is based upon the same principle which was clearly in operation in New Hampshire in 1883-1884.[4] This same experiment thus

[2] *Thirteenth Annual Catalog and Circular of the State Normal School*, pp. 11-12. 1883.
[3] *Ibid.*, pp. 9-12.
[4] Baker, Frank E. "Integrated Professional Experiences as the Basis for Learning and as a Substitute for Formal Courses in Education." *Yearbook of the American Association of Teachers Colleges*, pp. 70-85. 1933.

appears to have been tried more than fifty years ago. It will be interesting to follow this experiment down through the years, to note the manner in which it has persisted, and to study this practice in its more fully developed form under the more favorable conditions existing at later periods and at the present time.

In this curriculum is found a clear example of two developments in teacher education which are in some respects noteworthy. (*a*) This curriculum, unlike its predecessor, did not consist of reviews and drills in the common-school subjects. It took students immediately into new fields and presented material which they had not previously studied. The first three terms stressed subject matter which for those days and for the type of students who attended the normal school was advanced material. It was taught from the point of view of its use in teaching children. In the light of the fact that the majority of the students were only graduates of the district schools, probably from sixteen to eighteen years of age, the curriculum represented two years of liberal and cultural education of a desirable sort for persons with the attainments of such students. (*b*) Integrated professional experience as a basis for learning and as a substitute for formal courses in education provided an approach to methods through informal instruction by the critic teacher during the period of student teaching. This practice represented a clear recognition of the principle of functional learning in which each element in the learning situation is encountered in the setting in which it normally occurs. Students, as formerly, were admitted from the common schools; they were introduced immediately to the study of geometry, geology, and advanced work in English, and continued with algebra, physics, and more English. The curriculum was thus carried forward to a considerably higher level than that of the earliest curriculum established at the time of the founding of the institution. The most unique characteristic of this curriculum was the introduction of the full-time, all-day teaching with practically all pedagogical instruction given by the supervisor of student teaching informally and apart from any formal course in education.

If the character of the student body is kept in mind, the principles upon which this curriculum was based may be defended. The content of the various courses was described in considerable detail in the catalog. The first term of English included the study of composition together with wide reading in literature. It appeared to be an integrated course in literature and expression. It must be remembered that the amount of literature published in a form suitable for classroom study was limited at that time. Naturally the course failed to include a great deal which would be found in such a course at the present time. Nevertheless, the principle holds that it was an integrated course in English literature and expression. The second term developed into Milton, Macaulay, and Webster. The students' reading was directed by the instructor in English and a large amount of good literature was apparently read during the year. Composition was not set apart in a course by itself. The third term of twenty weeks was devoted to a "study of the development of reading and language during the twelve-year course in the public schools."[5] This last term's work was clearly a study of curriculum materials in English. Thus a very desirable sequence seems to have been established in this subject, consisting, first, of wide reading for background in literature combined with expression at appropriate times during the course, followed by pedagogical consideration of the course of study in English for the public schools, and culminating in the teaching of English in twenty weeks of full-time student teaching. It can hardly be denied that this was an advanced conception of the teaching of English when it is considered that it happened fifty years ago.

Mathematics included geometry, algebra, and commercial arithmetic. The last clearly meant a type of arithmetic in which applications to the practical affairs of life were studied in place of cube root, alligation, and similar topics. The work in mathematics culminated in a course in arithmetic, called elementary arithmetic, which included "the teaching to classes of children the facts, principles and processes involved in the work of the first five years."[6] This was clearly a study of curriculum materials, and, for the students in question, was based upon a solid foundation in mathematics.

A year's work in history included material selected from the whole field of world history, which seemed to give the best background for teachers' materials. The traditional course in United States history which already had been studied in the schools from which the students had come was not gone over in review; on the other hand, considerable study of American history was woven into the year's work in world history.[7]

Biological science was lacking, but other science included min-

[5] *Ibid.*, p. 11.   [6] *Ibid.*, p. 11.   [7] *Ibid.*, pp. 10-11.

eralogy, geology, geography, and physics. The last was an elementary course in physical science, restricted to the one field, but the method of teaching is interesting. "Pupils," it was said, in the description of the course, "are led to observe everyday phenomena in such a way as to teach the principle involved; they are also led to make and handle apparatus." The description of the list of topics studied concludes with the statement that "the subjects [topics] are taught pupils from the training school."[8] Evidently this was a course devoted to the teacher's background in physical science and the organization was made effective by teaching the materials to classes of children brought from the training school into the normal-school classroom. This plan of advanced study and concurrent organization of curriculum materials, with the actual teaching of those materials to children as a part of the normal school students' own learning and as a means of professionalizing the materials, represented a notable advance in the conception of teacher education.

It is not necessary to describe all the courses in detail. In general the same viewpoint prevailed through all the courses.

Under a new principal, the plan which has just been described was somewhat modified after a few years. New principles were introduced and certain of the former principles were retained and further developed. Some noteworthy advances were made and most of the gains in the previous curriculum were preserved. This was not a complete reorganization of the curriculum, but rather an extension of certain principles in what seemed at that time to be desirable directions.

The professional work, as it was called under this modified plan, was organized in a sequence which provided, in the first term, an introduction to schools and their organization and management. In later terms, mental philosophy, as it was called, and the science of education were discussed. Near the end of the curriculum, the history of education and systems of education were emphasized. A course in the art of teaching appeared in the last two terms. Student teaching, called training at that time, was carried throughout the six terms of the curriculum. The organization of the professional work, as it appeared in the catalog for 1884-1885, was as follows:[9]

---

[8] *Ibid.*, p. 11.
[9] *Fifteenth Annual Catalog and Circular of the New Hampshire State Normal School*, p. 17, 1884-1885.

FIRST YEAR

First Term	*Second Term*	*Third Term*
School Management	Mental Philosophy	Mental Philosophy
Training	Training	Science of Education
		Training

SECOND YEAR

Mental Philosophy	History of Education	Systems of Education
Science of Education	Art of Teaching	Art of Teaching
Training	Training	Training

Several aspects of this curriculum deserve consideration. The titles of the courses need to be translated into present-day terminology. It must be recalled, also, that materials available for courses in education in 1884-1885 were very different from those which could be brought into such courses two decades later or at the present time. One general fact about this work in education is that it clearly attempted to organize the materials into a suitable sequence extending from the time the student entered the normal school to the day of graduation. It also carried participation in the training school parallel with the study of education throughout the entire curriculum. It cannot be said, of course, that this work constituted the kind of an integrated sequence of work in education which has been proposed recently.[10] On the other hand, it can be said with equal positiveness that it undoubtedly represented the forerunner of such a sequence in education. Some aspects of this course in education are worthy of further consideration.

This concurrent study of the theory and principles of teaching and participation in the training school throughout the period of preparation was, for that day, a noteworthy advance in the practice of teacher education. It is clear that the participation was considered to be not an accompaniment of the course in education but an actual constituent of the course. Concerning this innovation the principal had this to say in his second report:

The training in teaching has been extended through a wider range. Pupils [students] now commence work in the training schools during the first term, and increase this amount from term to term. The training continues throughout the whole of the system—primary, grammar and high schools—and is so managed as to give training in methods of teaching, in the management of classes, and the management of schools. This work in training is done in

---

[10] Brown, H. A. "Essential Constituents of a Program for the Preparation of Elementary School Teachers." *Problems in Teacher Training*, 8: 140-159. New York: Prentice-Hall. 1934.

the schoolrooms, under conditions like those which will attend the work of the future teacher.[11]

The fact that the course in school management offered in the first term of the first year was an introduction to education has already been mentioned. This course included more than that term connotes at the present time in its restricted meaning. It dealt with the construction and furnishing of schoolhouses, but it also comprised a study of "modes of organization, gradation and management of schools."[12] Clearly this course presented a general picture of the organization of the kind of schools in which students would teach. It was apparently for the students of those days an appropriate introduction to the school as an institution. It was an introduction to education. The early work in training given in the first term with concurrent professional conferences was an introduction to teaching.

The ending of the sequence of work in education with the study of the history of education, especially systems of education, gave a second view of the system as a whole on a higher level of insight than was possible at the outset. This introduction to education at the beginning and this conclusion in a broadly conceived study of some aspects of the history of education and school systems might well meet with a good deal of approval at the present time. Some people now believe that a study of modern schools and their program and organization makes a fitting climax to a sequence of work in education. It is also advocated that a study of the history and philosophy of education should be taken up near the end of the curriculum. Undoubtedly the courses in history of education and systems of education included, for that time, such a viewpoint as is often advocated at the present time, but of course, with vastly restricted materials as compared with those available today.

SCIENCE FOR ELEMENTARY-SCHOOL TEACHERS

One other feature of the curriculum at this stage of its development deserves mention. From the beginning a great deal of attention was given to natural science in this curriculum.[13] The new cur-

[11] Rounds, Charles C. "Report of the Principal." *Annual Report of the State Normal School of New Hampshire*, p. 9. 1885.

[12] *Fifteenth Annual Catalog and Circular of the New Hampshire State Normal School*, p. 30. 1884-1885.

[13] *Fourth Annual Catalog of the Officers and Students of the New Hampshire State Normal School*, pp. 18-19. 1875.

riculum adopted in 1884-1885 contained a sequence in science which continued and developed the principle of science instruction for elementary-school teachers. Science was found in every term of the two-year period. This is the plan:

FIRST YEAR

First Term	Second Term	Third Term
Geography	Geography	Botany
Physics	Physics	

SECOND YEAR

Chemistry	Physiology	Physical Geography
Geology	Astronomy	

EARLY ATTEMPT TO PROFESSIONALIZE SUBJECT MATTER

This sequence amounted to a two-year course in the elements of the natural sciences with constant attention to the use of elementary-science materials in teaching in the lower schools. Similar sequences were carried through the two years in English language and literature and mathematics, including algebra, geometry, and bookkeeping. One term was devoted to civil government and one to political economy. History was accorded two terms, vocal music two terms, drawing two terms. "General Review of Elementary Studies" was found in the third term of the first year. This review was undoubtedly preparatory to the more responsible student teaching of the second year. It included recreation of scholarship at the point of teaching. It clearly appears that the ideal which dominated all this work was not academic. In discussing the purpose of the school the principal said:

. . . it must be borne in mind, that the instruction in subject matter is conducted with reference to methods of teaching, and that the ability of pupils [students] to teach what they are taught is developed and tested by practice. The attainment of this ability is the objective point in the work of the school, and the ultimate test of results. The point of view changes the aspect and character of the work, and no development of the work of the normal school can be called strictly academic.[14]

There was undoubtedly an attempt at this early date to professionalize subject matter. The content of the courses in the several so-called academic subjects was professionalized for use in teaching throughout the entire curriculum. No special courses in methods were offered at any time during the early period in this school.

[14] *Annual Report of the State Normal School of New Hampshire*, p. 26. 1885.

The curriculum as it appeared in 1892-1893 is given below.

This curriculum continued for nearly two decades without any very fundamental change in its form. A new conception of teacher education gradually began to develop in the institution, but the same curriculum was used. This new policy retained the concept of integration of psychology and theory and principles of teaching and concurrent experience in the training school.

Developments in psychology were taking place at this time. Dewey's conception of the nature and function of learning was

TWO-YEAR GENERAL CURRICULUM FOR ELEMENTARY-SCHOOL TEACHERS[15]

FIRST YEAR

	Semester Hours	
	First	Second
Field and Course	Semester	Semester
Education		
Psychology and Pedagogy with Observation in the Training Schools	2	
Psychology and Pedagogy with Observation in the Training Schools		3
English		
Reading	3	
Literature	3	
Writing	2	
Composition	3	
Grammar		3
English Literature		1
Social Science		
General History	3	
American History		3
Natural Science		
Natural History (Mineralogy, Geology, Zoology and Botany)	4	4
Geography		3
Physics		3
Mathematics		
Arithmetic	4	
Elements of Geometry	1	
Geometry		3
Art		
Drawing	2	2
	27	25

[15] *Twenty-third Annual Catalog and Circular of the New Hampshire State Normal School,* p. 19. 1892-1893.

SECOND YEAR

Field and Course	Semester Hours	
	First Semester	Second Semester
Education		
Pedagogy and Training	6	
Pedagogy and Training		9
English		
English Language and Literature	3	
Rhetoric		3
Social Science		
Civil Government and Law School	2	
History of Education		3
Natural Science		
Chemistry	3	
Physiology	4	
Physical Geography		5
Mathematics		
Algebra	4	
Bookkeeping and Review		4
Art		
Drawing	2	1
	24	25

coming into dominance. A little earlier the point of view in psychology represented by Hall and his followers had been influential. These and other aspects of education worked their way into the curriculum at Plymouth. Psychology represented a genetic approach to the study of child development and learning. Basic aspects of the theory of education were considered in connection with the study of psychology. Foundational work in psychology was done in the first semester and continued in the second with a gradual shift of emphasis to the theory of education and its application to teaching. Work in the training school was emphasized in the second semester and continued throughout the second year. While the course in education put a little more specific stress on genetic psychology at the outset, it continued, nevertheless, to be an integrated course in education from beginning to end with concurrent experience in the training school throughout the two years.[16]

This curriculum, in its slightly modified form but with a considerably altered conception, is presented next.

[16] *Fortieth Annual Catalog and Circular of the New Hampshire State Normal School*, p. 21. 1909-1910.

TWO-YEAR CURRICULUM FOR ELEMENTARY-SCHOOL TEACHERS[17]

FIRST YEAR

Field and Course	Semester Hours First Semester	Second Semester
Education		
Psychology (Genetic approach to child development and learning and basic aspects of theory of education)	4	
School Law	1	
Pedagogy and Observation (General theory of education and its application in teaching)		4
English		
English Composition (Individual instruction, original writing, papers in other courses, study of discourse structure)	3	3
Literature	3	3
Elocution (Voice training, pantomimes and recitals)	2	2
Social Science		
Current Topics	1	
European History		3
Natural Science		
Geography	2	2
Physiology	2	
Biology	3	
Chemistry		4
Mathematics		
Arithmetic	2	
Art		
Drawing	3	3
Music		
Music	2	2
Industrial Arts		
Manual Training		4
Health and Physical Education		
Physical Culture (Rhythm work, games, and theory of physical education)	4	
	—	—
	32	30

SECOND YEAR

Field and Course	Semester Hours First Semester	Second Semester
Education		
Pedagogy, Observation and Teaching (Theory of teaching and preliminary teaching in training school)	3	
History of Education		3

[17] *Ibid.*, p. 21.

Methods and Management (Problems in teaching and in classroom organization and management)........		2
Practice Teaching (Half-day teaching in the training school).......................................		*
English		
English Composition.............................	2	2
Literature (Study of literature of all times and selection of materials for children's language and reading)....	2	2
Elocution (Study of drama and production of plays, with emphasis on children's dramatics)...........	1	1
Social Science		
United States History and Civics..................	4	
Natural Science		
Physics...	4	
Mineralogy and Nature Study.....................	3	
Elementary Science (Curriculum and materials in science)......................................		3
Art		
Drawing..	2	2
Music		
Music..	2	2
Health and Physical Education		
Physical Culture................................	4	
	27	17

This curriculum continued the principle which was found in former curricula. It did not place emphasis on reteaching the common branches of the elementary school. This declaration is found in the catalog:

... the policy of the school is not to duplicate any work done in other schools of the state. All studies completed in colleges, accredited high schools or accredited academies will be accepted.[18]

In place of studying the elementary-school subjects in review courses an attempt was made to enter upon more advanced work at the start. The work in science in earlier curricula was continued, but students who had had equivalent work were excused from any course in science.[19] The two-year sequence in English literature and composition continued the practice noted in earlier curricula. Art, music, and industrial arts were new subjects for most of the students. Elocution, as it was called at that time, was work in speech. It took students into the field of voice study and drama and

[18] *Fortieth Annual Catalog and Circular of the New Hampshire State Normal School*, p. 18. 1909-1910.
[19] *Ibid.*, p. 21.

included voice training for public speaking; pantomimes and recitals; study of dramatic selections from Shakespeare, Browning, Tennyson, Rossetti, Kipling, and others; theater training and production of plays.[20] Nature study included the life histories of plants and animals as a preparation for teaching nature study, school gardening, and elementary agriculture in the schools.[21] It was an integrated course in practical biological science as a background for teachers. In physics and chemistry it was said that "such topics are taken up as will be likely to aid teachers in their future work."[22] This was a teacher's background course in general physical science. The last course, entitled "Elementary Science" and taken concurrently with practice teaching, was clearly a course in the organization of curriculum materials.[23]

The conception of the work in art which prevailed is representative of the practices which were in operation at that time. This is what the catalog said about it:

... It is the aim of this department to lead the pupils [students] to an appreciation of beauty in nature and art, to realize the value and importance of drawing, to use drawing as an aid in other studies, thus making a close correlation with all the other subjects in the curriculum. The work is classified under these heads:

Pictorial drawing or representation, includes the study and application of the principles to the drawing of the objects and of plant and animal life, also landscape composition. For illustrative drawing there is an abundance of material in literature, history, geography.

Decoration includes the study of the principles of design, the theory and the harmony of colors, the history of art and the application of these principles to the study and the selection of the art decoration and color schemes for home and school decoration.

Structural drawing includes the study of drawings and the application of art principles to the construction of objects.

Blackboard sketching and chalk modeling are very important in the course. The pupils [students] learn to sketch freely and quickly on the blackboard illustrations of the various subjects of school work.

The application and correlation of drawing to the work of all grades is carefully studied. The pupils [students] plan outlines, lessons, or give lessons adapted to the grades. They also learn to use the different mediums adapted to school use. This includes work in water color, pencil, crayon, chalk, charcoal and pen and ink.[24]

Music followed the same general plan, so the content of the courses

[20] *Ibid.*, p. 17.   [22] *Ibid.*, p. 16.
[21] *Ibid.*, p. 16.   [23] *Ibid.*, p. 16.
[24] *Fortieth Annual Catalog and Circular of the New Hampshire State Normal School*, pp. 14-15. 1919-1920.

will not be described in full. It included sight singing; elements of musical form; ear training; elementary music theory; chorus practice, including development of rhythmic sense, expression and interpretation, part singing, and acquaintance with the best musical literature. At the end of the sequence presentation of music in the schoolroom was emphasized as well as collection and preparation of necessary materials. Observation of work in music in the training school was especially emphasized. The work in practice teaching included the teaching of music.[25]

Manual training, as taught at this normal school at this time, had largely broken away from the formality which earlier, and even at that time, characterized such work in most places. The educational aspects of the subject were stressed. It was said of manual training:

In all this work the object is not the creation of more or less useful or ornamental bits of bric-a-brac, toys or furniture, not the acquirement of a certain skill or proficiency in handling the tools of any particular craft or trade, and not the limited training for vocational work, which is popularly and erroneously thought to be the aim. . . . Our object is rather the uniform development of the individual . . . and to infuse the pupil [student] with an appreciation of the dignity and the joy of work, with a sense of glory in achievement, and with a realization of power. This aim utilizes the natural tendency of every young boy or girl to activity of body, and organizes it to the accomplishment of something definite. The wood and the leather, the iron and the raffia are only the objective focal points, the finished birdhouse, pocket or coin purse only the by-products of this organized activity, which has as its major product brains, motor adjustment, moral fibre and the joy of living and working.[26]

It is clear that the work in manual training consisted of a series of projects, for it was said that:

The problems for execution are graded from simple household articles and toys for beginners to small pieces of furniture for the older and more skilled students.[27]

Physical culture, as it was called, included rhythm work, games, and general instruction in the theory of gymnastics. Geography included (a) general geography studied through the things near at hand: surface forms, drainage, soil, climate, products, and industries, as applied to town and state; (b) comparative geography of the continents, using North America as a type.[28]

It is apparent that class recitations were given before the school

[25] *Ibid.*, p. 15.
[26] *Ibid.*, p. 17.
[27] *Ibid.*, p. 16.
[28] *Ibid.*, p. 18.

and criticized by students and teachers.[29]   Students prepared written analyses and plans of lessons for such criticism.   Teaching exercises were conducted by normal-school teachers before classes and before the school and were critically discussed by students and teachers with written statements of the results of the discussions made by students in turn.[30]   Concerning these exercises it was said that

. . . These exercises are given to normal school classes, or to classes from the training schools, and are frequently assigned to a class or a section of a class to prepare, one of the number being designated, after the preparation, to give the exercise.[31]

This curriculum continued in the general form in which it is quoted throughout the remainder of the first period of the history of teacher education in New Hampshire.   It was not changed in any significant manner until Morrison made a comprehensive reorganization. It was an evolving curriculum and for that reason it did not remain in exactly the same form through any period of two or three years.

This curriculum in its final form in 1909-1910 exhibited a number of features which are worthy of discussion.   The unbroken sequence of courses in special fields, which prevailed all through this period, represented an early development in teacher education which has received a great deal of emphasis in recent years.   This statement has special reference to subject-matter courses.   They were organized into compact programs of work and an attempt was made to provide content best adapted to the needs of teachers.   The type of science, history, mathematics, and similar subjects which was found in liberal arts colleges and which was taken over by normal schools to some extent, never found its way into the curriculum of the New Hampshire normal schools.   In these courses there was an increasing tendency to organize near the end of each sequence suitable curriculum materials for use in teaching in the various grades.   This did not preclude, however, pedagogical treatment of the various subjects at every step.   An important fact about these courses was that continuity of learning was sought and obtained in these coherent groups into which the various courses were organized.   A given subject, like biological and physical science, was so organized as to provide for consecutive study throughout two years in a continuous and to some extent unified sequence of subject matter, which constituted a comprehensive field of study.   It is true that the work was organized in the form of a series of courses instead of a single

[29] *Ibid.*, p. 12.   [30] *Ibid.*, p. 12.   [31] *Ibid.*, p. 12.

integrated course. On the other hand, a desirable continuity and sequence prevailed. The curriculum, as a whole, represented an attempt to organize the various subjects into a limited number of fields which were studied somewhat comprehensively through these groups of sequential and related courses in each field. It culminated in a single course which aimed at a somewhat extensive grasp of the curriculum materials of the whole field. For example, the sequence of courses in science ended with a course in elementary science. Even though all the materials of the several courses were professionalized from the beginning, nevertheless a final integration and professionalization took place in this course in curriculum materials. The final course accompanied student teaching.

PART III

REORGANIZATION AND PROGRESS IN TEACHER EDUCATION UNDER INCREASING CENTRALIZATION

CHAPTER IV

ADOPTION OF A STATE-WIDE POLICY AND PROGRAM OF TEACHER EDUCATION

AT THE beginning of his administration in 1904 Morrison began to study the question of demand for teachers and available supply. This problem had not been studied in any extensive way before that time and practically no literature on the subject was then available. Morrison proceeded to assemble in the next few years by scientific methods a great amount of pertinent factual material on this problem. He thus plowed new ground in this field. His studies were published in his several biennial reports. In the first report he made an estimate of the number of new teachers needed annually in the state. In the second year of the first biennium he found 376 elementary-school teachers teaching for the first time in the state. He took that number to represent the annual number of new teachers needed. He found that 46 had been graduated that year at the state normal school and that 35 of these were teaching in the state. Accurate data were not available, but he estimated that 300 of the new teachers were without professional preparation. Some were high-school graduates and a large number were uneducated and totally without professional preparation.[1]

Morrison estimated the teacher needs of the state by determining the number of teachers without experience who were employed each year. More recently "new" teachers have been defined as the number of teachers new to their positions in any given year. Thus in the case of a teacher who changed from one position to another within the state both that teacher and his or her successor would be "new" teachers, but only one position required a teacher not previously employed in the state. Morrison found that a good many teachers came to New Hampshire from other states. Some came directly from normal schools and some from other positions in those states. The number of inexperienced teachers who were employed

---

[1] Morrison, Henry C. *Report of the Superintendent of Public Instruction*, p. 185. 1906.

annually in the state seemed to Morrison to represent the problem of the state teacher-education institutions. He found that for a ten-year period an average of 355 such teachers had been required, with 257 and 378 as the extremes.[2]

In his first biennial report, Morrison referred to the quality of teachers who were at work in the public school system. He found in the elementary schools 75 college graduates, 476 normal school graduates, 381 graduates of city training schools, 1,213 who were graduates of high schools or academies but without further education, and 467 with no higher education than that afforded by the elementary schools. They were usually products of the poorest elementary schools. From an inspection of the schools, and from the results of tests which he gave, Morrison concluded that not more than one teacher in three was properly prepared for his work. He called eighteen per cent utterly incompetent both academically and professionally.[3] This was only a preliminary estimate and was not based upon a thorough analysis of the whole teacher situation. It was not until he had entered upon the second biennium of his administration that Morrison approached the problem for the purpose of making a thorough analysis.

In 1908 Morrison made a comprehensive analysis of the situation with reference to the preparation of teachers in the elementary schools of the state. His first object was to find the facts. His was one of the first effective studies of supply and demand in this country. This was eighteen years before Buckingham published his study of supply and demand in Ohio.[4] It was eight years before the survey of teacher needs in the state of Missouri.[5] Morrison realized, as did Learned and Bagley later, that "selection and management of professional curricula cannot proceed intelligently without a fairly exact knowledge of the dimensions of the problem to be solved."[6] In a survey of the teaching positions in the state, Morrison found these facts:

[2] Morrison, Henry C. *Report of the Superintendent of Public Instruction of New Hampshire*, p. 323. 1908.

[3] Morrison, Henry C. *Report of the Superintendent of Public Instruction*, p. 185. 1906.

[4] Buckingham, B. R. *Supply and Demand in Teacher Training.* Bureau of Educational Research Monographs, No. 4. Columbus, Ohio: Ohio State University Studies. 1926.

[5] Learned, William S., Bagley, William C., and Others. *The Professional Preparation of Teachers for American Public Schools*, pp. 265-271. 1920.

[6] *Ibid.*, p. 265.

2,529 elementary school teachers in the state.

 401 with little or no preparation beyond the elementary schools, which in most cases meant the one-room rural schools.

 471 graduates of normal schools.

 384 graduates of city training schools

  76 college graduates.

1,197 graduates of high schools or academies, but not of normal schools.[7]

Thus it appeared that of the 2,529 elementary-school teachers in the state about 1,600 or nearly two-thirds of the total teaching staff were without minimum preparation for their work. This represented to Morrison the extent of the problem which had to be solved in order to place a professionally prepared teacher in every rural and urban elementary schoolroom in the state of New Hampshire. All this represented very substantial fact-finding, rare at that time, as a basis for procedure in teacher education.

AVAILABLE FACILITIES FOR TEACHER PREPARATION

The next step was to discover what facilities the state had for solving the problem. It was found that the one state normal school had graduated annually during the past five years an average of 37 students who were high-school graduates with one or two years of professional preparation beyond the secondary school. For the five-year period under consideration, 13 was the average number of graduates with one year of professional preparation. They were mostly experienced teachers, who might or might not be high-school graduates, and who were admitted to a one-year curriculum on the basis of their experience. Thus the state was getting from its own state normal school fewer than 25 graduates a year who were high-school graduates with two additional years of professional preparation.[8]

There seemed to be no prospect of any materially greater number of graduates at the one state normal school. The school was located in a small village with only the village schools for training purposes. It did not seem possible, at that time, to secure additional facilities which would permit a much larger enrollment. Other states with more normal schools were the only other source of supply of professionally prepared teachers. Morrison did not see any particular

---

[7] Morrison, Henry C. "Securing an Efficient Teaching Force—Some Things Which Must Be Observed." *Report of the State Superintendent of Public Instruction*, p. 334. 1908.

[8] *Ibid.*, pp. 322-325.

possibilities in near-by schools, for salaries were higher in adjoining states, and those states were no more than supplying their own demands, and in some cases were even failing to do that. The situation, then, in New Hampshire was this: (a) an annual demand for 355 inexperienced elementary-school teachers with two years of preparation beyond secondary schools; (b) an annual supply of 25 graduates from the one state normal school.

Analyzing the problem, this meant that the state needed at that time fourteen times as many new professionally prepared elementary-school teachers as it was getting in order to fill vacancies with teachers who had the desired minimum academic and professional preparation. This figure took no account of the supply of teachers needed gradually to replace 1,600 unqualified elementary-school teachers then teaching in the state. If these were to be replaced at the rate of 50 a year, the state really needed sixteen times as many normal-school graduates as it was then receiving from the state normal school.

SOCIAL SIGNIFICANCE OF TEACHER EDUCATION

In this situation, the actual relative numbers were small, but the problem was nevertheless one of large proportions. The elementary schools of the state were supposed to provide for all citizens that foundational preparation for citizenship which was believed to be an absolute essential as a basis for an enlightened public opinion. The problem appeared in exactly this light to Morrison, and it was not surprising that he bent every energy to its solution. In fact it seemed so important that for the first few years of his administration the preparation of secondary-school teachers received little attention.

In his second biennial report, Morrison surveyed the situation with reference to the preparation of teachers in the high schools and academies. He found 323 regular teachers employed in approved secondary schools. Of these, 286 were college graduates. The others had specially approved preparation for their work, such as European study in preparation for teaching modern foreign languages. The competency of these teachers did not appear to be great except that they had an academic education of the traditional sort provided at the time by colleges and universities. Their academic background was not professionalized in the manner now deemed desirable. They had taken no courses in education.

ADVOCACY OF ADDITIONAL MEANS FOR TEACHER EDUCATION

In general, the attack on the problem of teacher education during Morrison's administration went forward in two different directions: (a) a movement was immediately started to provide the state with more normal schools; (b) the development of a school of education at the state university was advocated. Morrison founded his arguments upon substantial factual data which were the results of his researches and also upon certain fundamental principles pertinent to the New Hampshire situation at that time. These principles still have a wide and significant application in the field of teacher education. They were commented upon at some length in a government publication issued in 1916.[9] Morrison organized a long-time program designed eventually to place in every classroom in the state an educated and professionally prepared teacher. As a basis for his procedures he made further intensive studies of the problem.

ANALYSIS OF SERVICE OF TEACHER-EDUCATION INSTITUTIONS

By a preliminary study made in 1906-1907, shortly after his appointment, Morrison gathered convincing evidence that the sections of the state which received little or no service from the state normal school in the form of professionally prepared teachers were those areas which were remote from Plymouth where the one normal school was located. The counties near the normal school were sparsely settled. More distant counties had the largest resources in wealth and population but they contributed few students to the normal school.[10]

PRINCIPLE OF TEACHER-EDUCATION AREAS IN THE STATE

The obvious conclusion from the conditions then existing in New Hampshire was that each section of the state must produce as many professionally prepared teachers as it needed to recruit its own teaching force. As the basis for planning at that time in New Hampshire, it was postulated that any region remote from a teacher-education institution would have difficulty in providing itself with the

[9] Judd, Charles H. and Parker, Samuel C. *Problems Involved in Standardizing State Normal Schools.* Washington, D. C.: Bureau of Education, Bulletin No. 12. 1916.
[10] Morrison, Henry C. *Report of the Superintendent of Public Instruction of New Hampshire,* pp. 326-327. 1908.

best quality of personnel in its teaching staff. Generally speaking, it was declared, the best of each graduating class from any teacher-education institution would find positions near home and only those who found difficulty in securing positions in their own localities would migrate to distant regions. It seemed necessary, therefore, that each area in the state should prepare its own teachers. With normal schools accessible, it would be easier to induce the best members of high-school graduating classes to attend normal schools. Thus it would be more likely that the best native stock could be educated for teaching. This principle was clearly stated as the basis for whatever procedures were introduced in solving the teacher-education problem as Morrison conceived it.[11]

It would not necessarily hold that every teacher would go back to the same town or even the same area in the state from which he or she came. Teachers might often go to other states and other teachers might come from outside the state. This seemed to Morrison to be desirable so far as a certain proportion of the teaching staff of the state was concerned. It did seem desirable, nevertheless, that every section should produce as many teachers as it annually received. This was one foundation-principle upon which Morrison built. The period at which he was writing was one in which transportation was more difficult than now. Good roads had not been developed and the motor vehicle had not come into general use. The teacher-education areas within a state as Morrison projected them may be larger under modern facilities for travel. The general principle, however, in the judgment of the present writer, applies to modern states as clearly as it did nearly thirty years ago in New Hampshire. It is undoubtedly true at the present time that, in order to maintain a stable and sufficient staff of teachers with the highest qualifications, every state must educate its own quota. In large states the several sections must do the same. Morrison enunciated, therefore, and emphasized what is generally recognized as a fundamental principle of state administration of teacher education.

FIVE TEACHER-EDUCATION ZONES

An investigation made by Morrison revealed five natural centers in the state with such annual teacher needs that a normal school located centrally in each of these areas with a given enrollment could

[11] Morrison, Henry C. *Report of the Superintendent of Public Education*, p. 149. 1912.

supply every vacancy in the state with a professionally prepared teacher. The average annual need for new teachers in each of these areas was carefully computed; the enrollment in each normal school needed to supply the teacher requirements of the section was determined. The cities which had school systems large enough to furnish adequate training schools for the enrollments contemplated were named. It was no part of the plan to locate these new normal schools, as has been done in a good many cases, in the towns or cities which bid the highest or which had the greatest political influence.[12] The whole plan of establishing normal schools was based upon the needs of the state for service as revealed in fact-finding studies, and not upon any political expediency. Normal schools were not to be given to the highest bidder. Teacher education was conceived to be a state function; it was to be conducted in such a manner as to render the necessary service to the state. Normal schools did not exist for the personal benefit of young people who desired to teach. Their sole reason for existence was to furnish the state with the necessary number of competent teachers. In this respect they differed in purpose from institutions for general education. Every normal school, it was held, should be so located as to furnish the best prospect of enabling a section of the state to provide itself with professionally prepared teachers.[13]

The plan for five normal-school zones[14] in the state, at the center of each of which it was deemed necessary to place a state normal school, was intended to enable the state to furnish professionally prepared teachers for all its schools. The railroad lines, the population, the topography of the state, and other similar factors determined the extent and character of the zones. The five zones were:

a. The Plymouth zone in the center of the state—a relatively long, narrow area along the line of a railroad which extended throughout the length of the state.

b. The southwestern area, with the city of Keene at its center, and with railroad lines radiating in several directions, resembling somewhat a circle with the normal school at its center.

c. The southeastern section, the largest and most populous area in the state, with several cities which had railroad and interurban

[12] Humphreys, Harry C. *Factors Operating in the Location of State Normal Schools.* New York: Bureau of Publications, Teachers College, Columbia University. 1922.

[13] Morrison, Henry C. *Op. cit.*, p. 151. 1912.

[14] *Ibid.*, pp. 135-151.

electric lines extending in several directions into the outlying parts of the area.

d. The northern area, a remote section in the northern part of the state with a railroad extending north into the heart of the most northerly portion of the state and two railroad lines extending south into the central zone and southeast into the southeastern area.

e. The south central section, along the line of a railroad which extended the length of the state, with several lateral branch railroads and containing the three largest cities in the state.

The care with which Morrison planned is shown in his analysis of normal-school needs. He had data to show that at the time the state required two normal schools of 150 students each, two of 250 students, and one of 350 students.[15]

PLANNING IN TERMS OF EXACT KNOWLEDGE OF TEACHER NEEDS

As a result of the careful studies which this zoning of the state involved, charts were at hand showing the exact source of each student in the normal schools and the location of each graduate. On the basis of such data kept for a period of years it was possible to do such effective planning as has been described. Such statements as the following show the nature of this planning:

Beginning with Plymouth and continuing outward, town by town, we find that 70 new teachers annually are required in a territory extending from Concord on the south to Littleton on the north, and including all rural towns in Grafton, Merrimack, and Carroll Counties, which are accessible to Plymouth.

Now, when this territory reaches the point that it will provide itself with trained teachers, it will tax Plymouth more and more to its full capacity.[16]

Again:

Coos County needs from 30 to 40 inexperienced trained teachers annually, and this rises from 50 to 60 if we come down to the edge of the natural Plymouth territory at Littleton and down the line of the Maine Central Railroad to, say, Conway in Carroll County. . . . Berlin could train an enrollment of about three hundred fifty; Lancaster about one hundred fifty; Colebrook about one hundred.[17]

[15] Morrison, Henry C. *Report of the Superintendent of Public Instruction*, p. 325. 1908.
[16] Morrison, Henry C. *Report of the Superintendent of Public Instruction*, pp. 148. 1912.
[17] *Ibid.*, pp. 148-149.

Another:

> This territory requires about one hundred twenty new teachers annually
> which indicates the need of a [normal] school with a maximum enrollment
> of approximately three hundred.
> Dover has material for training an enrollment of approximately four hun-
> dred thirty-five; Portsmouth an enrollment of five hundred twenty-five;
> Rochester one of three hundred ninety.[18]

In no other state at that time had planning of this kind ever been
done in teacher education.[19] It represented proceeding in terms of
a comprehensive factual analysis of the whole situation by the chief
educational officer of the state whose interest in public education
impelled him to seek whatever measures would advance the educational welfare of the state. Political considerations did not constitute the basis for decisions. Institutional and regional ambitions
were not the determiners of action. The problem was an educational
one and it was considered on such grounds.

When a new state normal school was established at Keene in
1908, its tendencies were studied in order to confirm or reject the
guiding principles which had been established for the location of
future normal schools. Morrison's figures for Keene revealed that
the graduates returned in general to the same restricted area from
which they had come.[20] It was found that 75 per cent of the class
of 1913 and 63 per cent of the class of 1914, or 71 per cent of the
two classes combined, returned to the same restricted area from
which they came.[21] At the same time it was discovered that, while
Plymouth graduates were more widely scattered, nevertheless, 61
per cent of the class of 1913 whose addresses were known went to
the zone from which that school drew 61 per cent of its enrollment.[22]

All this discussion of the teacher-education problem represented
planning in terms of exact knowledge of the teacher needs of the
state. It contemplated planned and restricted enrollments which
would furnish all the schools of the state with professionally prepared teachers, but at the same time would provide no more than a
desirable surplus.

---

[18] *Ibid.*, pp. 149-150.
[19] Judd, Charles H., and Parker, Samuel C. *Op. cit.*, p. 12.
[20] Morrison, Henry C. *Report of the Superintendent of Public Instruction*, p.
153. 1914.
[21] *Ibid.*, p. 153.
[22] *Ibid.*, p. 154.

IMPERATIVE NEED OF ADEQUATE TRAINING SCHOOL
FACILITIES

Fundamental principles based upon factual studies were sought as guides in all discussions and action with reference to the preparation of teachers. For example, it was considered especially important to locate normal schools only in places where there was a sufficient enrollment in the elementary schools to provide adequate facilities for participation and student teaching. Morrison considered five normal schools sufficient at that time. Furthermore his investigations and studies convinced him that normal schools must be small institutions. This conviction was based upon two hypotheses. First, it was necessary to have abundant training-school facilities. That presented a very great difficulty whenever normal schools became very large institutions. Second, the philosophy upon which Morrison built placed great dependence upon experience as a factor in learning in teacher education. This fact made necessary extensive training-school opportunities for participation in the actual work of schools throughout the entire period of preparation to an extent not generally accepted at that time.[23] It was held that such an understanding of the theory and principles of teaching as would be a guide to a teacher in his or her growth in self-dependence could be acquired only through the use of such theory and principles in teaching. Principles, it was held, could be understood only by using them. The idea was expressed in these words:

The broad intellectual foundation derived from the study of the principles of pedagogy and of education is essential to the capacity of the future teacher for growth and for independent work. Practice in applying those principles under the eye of the best teachers obtainable is essential to the right knowledge of the principles themselves, and still more essential to the practical efficiency of the teacher when she takes her first school. As in all other workers, so in the teacher, theory is a necessary foundation, but practical knowledge is essential to success. Now, if you increase the attendance at a normal school above and beyond the capacity of the model school to provide opportunity for practice, you lay the axe at the root of the power of the whole school to turn out practical teachers. A normal school must then in its location be in connection with a system of public schools large enough to afford sufficient opportunity for practice. Located in a village, its size will manifestly soon reach the limitations imposed by the village schools.[24]

[23] *Ibid.*, pp. 325-326.
[24] Morrison, Henry C. *Report of the Superintendent of Public Instruction of New Hampshire*, p. 199. 1906.

These reasons as well as others made it seem best to establish several small normal schools in order that training facilities might be adequate. The example of the very large normal schools in other parts of the country which had training schools with fewer pupils than they had students in the normal school itself seemed to Morrison to represent a fundamentally wrong principle. If participation in actual schools in teaching and in other kinds of work which a teacher does were essential to a complete understanding of the theory and principles of teaching, one large central normal school did not meet the requirements. The added fact was taken into consideration that in those times it would not draw a sufficient number of students from every part of the state to enable it to return to each section the necessary number of teachers.[25]

REQUIREMENTS GOVERNING LOCATION OF NORMAL SCHOOLS

Three essential requirements were especially emphasized. Morrison held that normal schools needed to be located in large population centers with good railroad connections, in sections as remote as possible from existing normal schools, and in cities large enough to furnish abundant training-school facilities.[26]

GRADUAL DISAPPEARANCE OF DECENTRALIZATION

Until 1919 the New Hampshire normal schools had a separate board of trustees, consisting of the governor, the state superintendent, and five other members appointed by the governor and council. The state superintendent, who was secretary of the board, was its executive officer in the control and management of the state normal schools. This was accomplished as a policy of the board of trustees. Thus was established the principle of direct control and supervision of state normal schools by the state department of public instruction, even under a separate board of trustees of which the state superintendent was only an *ex-officio* member in whom resided no direct statutory power over normal schools.

During this period, therefore, the normal schools were at all times under the close supervision of the state department of public instruction. The state superintendent personally acted as director of teacher education. He visited normal schools frequently for

[25] *Ibid.*, pp. 198-199.
[26] Morrison, Henry C. *Report of the Superintendent of Public Instruction of New Hampshire*, p. 325. 1908.

purposes of supervision. During the years 1913-1917 a deputy state superintendent of public instruction, in the capacity of what would now be called director of teacher training, visited each of the state normal schools at least four times each year and usually spent an entire week at the larger normal school on a single visit. In the biennium 1914-1916 eight such thorough inspections of each state normal school were made. Thus both normal schools and the training schools were surveyed and inspected with thoroughness and frequency.[27] The principle of complete control and close supervision of the state normal schools by the state was established during the four years beginning in 1913, and has been continued to the present time. These facts indicate centralization of control and direction through educational leadership rather than by statutory provisions.

STATE CONTROL WITHOUT MANAGEMENT OR ADMINISTRATION

State control, however, did not go into the details of management of the schools nor did it take away the initiative of the principals in administering and developing the institutions under their charge. In his first report, Morrison stated that the principal of the state normal school had been made the financial agent of the board of trustees in all matters. It appeared, also, that the board acted under the advice of the principal and committed to his hands the details of administration.[28] The principal was given a free hand in creating and maintaining a faculty. He and his faculty determined the policy of the school.[29] Thus from the beginning of centralization the principle of freedom in administration under policies determined by the board but on the initiative of the principal and his faculty was maintained and it has never been abrogated.

[27] Morrison, Henry C. "Condition of the State Normal Schools." *Report of the Superintendent of Public Instruction*, p. 194. 1916.
[28] Morrison, Henry C. *Report of the Superintendent of Public Instruction of New Hampshire*, pp. 197-198. 1906.
[29] Morrison, Henry C. *Report of the Superintendent of Public Instruction of New Hampshire*, p. 203. 1908.

CHAPTER V

REORGANIZATION AND EXTENSION OF THE PROGRAM FOR THE EDUCATION OF ELEMENTARY-SCHOOL TEACHERS

IMPRESSED as he was with the task which confronted the elementary school, it was but natural that Morrison should attach very great importance to the preparation of elementary-school teachers. After analyzing the problem, he established a long-time program and set himself resolutely to its consummation. A thoroughgoing reorganization and extension of the program for the education of elementary-school teachers was accomplished in the later years of his administration. This reconstruction involved a fundamental change in the policies governing teacher education. The new program was worked out in conferences with the heads of the two normal schools, the members of the state education department, and selected members of the faculties of the two normal schools. In general, however, the conception which prevailed in the new curriculum was formulated more generally by Morrison than by any other single person. It represented very completely his philosophy of teacher education. This reorganization involved teacher-education principles which are significant and which have value as a basis for considering ends and purposes as well as procedures in the preparation of teachers.

THEORY AND RELATED EXPERIENCE IN THE NORMAL-SCHOOL CURRICULUM

Morrison thought of the normal-school curriculum as consisting of six fields for study. Each had a part which was considered to be theory, and another which was conducted as practice. The two aspects of each field were carried on concurrently and were merely two phases of the same activity. Practice as Morrison interpreted it was experience. He listed five of the six elements of the curriculum thus conceived in two parallel columns in which he indicated that part of each which was theory and, under practice, that which was experience.[1] The curriculum, which was based upon this analysis, broke sharply with most normal-school curricula of that day or any more recent period.

The elements of the curriculum, as formulated by Morrison, and their organization into a normal-school program of studies need to be explained at this point. First, then, the main constituents of the normal-school curriculum set out in parallel columns, as Morrison organized them, will be presented. Second, an actual curriculum of one of the normal schools will be reproduced to show how these curriculum elements worked out in an actual program.

ELEMENTS IN THE NORMAL-SCHOOL CURRICULUM[2]

I. PSYCHOLOGY AND PEDAGOGY

Theory	*Practice*
General educational psychology; psychology of the primary school subjects; psychological tests; adolescent psychology (for those who took a third year in preparation for teaching in the junior high school); theory related to teaching situations and especially to the use of subject matter.	Classroom observation; practice teaching; methodology of elementary school subjects; practice teaching and methodological study of subject matter of algebra and geometry, elementary science, literature, music, agriculture, drawing, domestic arts, Latin, French. Of the last seven subjects, three were to be chosen.

II. SCHOOL MANAGEMENT

Theory	*Practice*
Brief course in school law; organization of school and theory of use of program and time table; habits and routine; work, fatigue, and interest; testing and marking; grading and promotion; attendance work; school records; sanitation; and similar topics.	Practice in school management; conferences and criticisms; conduct of various routine aspects of the work of the school from the beginning as an apprentice in the various classrooms of the training school; emphasis on understanding.

III. PHYSICAL EDUCATION

Theory	*Practice*
Physical nature and development of the child; plays and games; folk and natural dancing; corrective gymnastics.	Observation; study; measurements; experience in the training schools; and at the same time class work in the same subjects on the level of the normal school students.

[1] Morrison, Henry C. "Condition of the State Normal Schools." *Report of the Superintendent of Public Instruction*, pp. 204-205.

[2] *Ibid.*, pp. 204-205.

IV. INDUSTRIAL AND FINE ARTS

Theory	Practice
Educational meaning and relations.	Observation and practice teaching in art, drawing, and industrial arts.

V. EDUCATIONAL SOCIOLOGY

Theory	Practice
Dependent, defective and delinquent classes and corrective laws and institutions; race history and social conditions of race elements of New Hampshire population; social justification of different subjects in the program.	Study and observation in the practice schools; theses which involved a good deal of original investigation of special problems connected with the characteristics of the racial stocks in the New Hampshire population.

VI. ACADEMIC STUDIES

The heads of the normal schools were expected to ascertain the preliminary education of students and assign those who needed it to work in nature study, domestic arts, manual training, drawing, music, elementary science, and (elective) agriculture.

The materials which were included in some of these fields were different twenty years ago from the content which is now found in such courses. The important thing about this new curriculum is that it included every phase in both its theoretical aspect and its experience aspect. This curriculum thus acknowledged a fundamental principle: it recognized the function and place of concurrent experience as a factor in learning in all phases of teacher education. It assumed that students learn with experience. It sought and obtained a type of organization based upon that principle. It brought the training school into the picture to an extent which, at that time, was not general and even at the present time does not characterize many teachers colleges. The courses in education were believed to have their foundation in experience: accordingly broad and deep experience was made the basis for learning to the greatest extent possible. The writer has searched through catalogs of teachers colleges of the early period in an effort to discover another as complete and early an example of the union of theory and experience in the education of teachers extending throughout an entire curriculum. This search failed to reveal an earlier example of such a practice in such complete operation in an entire state.

A CURRICULUM PROFESSIONALIZED FROM THE BEGINNING

Another conception of teacher education appeared in this curriculum. It was assumed that the academic aspect of subjects taught in the elementary and the secondary schools had been studied sufficiently for the purposes of general education. For that reason no academic subjects except those not generally taught in the elementary and the secondary schools were included in the normal-school curriculum. Separate courses were not offered in English grammar, English composition, children's literature, arithmetic, history, and similar subjects taught in isolation as academic subjects. The normal school, according to Morrison's conception, was considered to be a professional school. It was assumed that the elementary schools and the high schools had done their work so far as academic preparation in the subjects studied there was concerned. Those schools were, to a large extent, under the control of the state department of public instruction. The remedy for any failure was believed to lie in improvements in those schools rather than in reteaching their work in the normal school. It was assumed, for example, that eight or nine years of study of English composition in the elementary school and four more in the secondary school had produced a student with enough basic academic command of elementary English writing and its principles to enter immediately upon the study of the professional aspects of teaching children to write English. If that was not the case, it was not likely that three hours a week of additional study of the subject for a year in the normal school would produce such a person.[3] The assumption applied to the other subjects, such as arithmetic, history, spelling, and writing.

Morrison set forth his conception underlying this curriculum when he said "the normal school is a place for professional training and not one for general education."[4] As far as the work of the normal schools, apart from the training school, was concerned, Morrison recognized but two aspects, expressed in his own language as follows:

First, there is the normal school proper, in which instruction in the principles of education, pedagogy, and school management is given.

[3] Doudna, Edgar G. "English in Teachers Colleges." *Educational Administration and Supervision*, 18: 31-34. January, 1932.
[4] Morrison. *Op. cit.*, p. 198.

Second, practice teaching in which students give instruction to the children under oversight for one-half day each for a total of eighteen weeks.[5]

Another statement of Morrison shows the limits which were set upon the instruction:

Instruction in the theory and practice of teaching is . . . limited to such principles as find application in the daily life of the room teacher and which may be exemplified in the practice school.[6]

In announcing this new curriculum in his biennial report in 1916, Morrison stated one of the fundamental principles upon which it was based. That principle showed the emphasis which was placed upon practice and the relationship of practice and theory in the actual operation of the curriculum. This is his statement:

Theory and practice are to be carried on nearly simultaneously. Each class will be divided into two or more divisions. Each division will begin with practice for three months, followed by theory for three months, followed by practice for three months.[7]

As a matter of fact, the alternating periods of theory and practice were nine-week periods, so that each student had in the second year eighteen weeks of work which was predominantly theory, and another period of equal length devoted chiefly to practice. This was the arrangement for the two groups:

| I. | Teaching for nine weeks | Study for nine weeks | Teaching for nine weeks | Study for nine weeks |
| II. | Study for nine weeks | Teaching for nine weeks | Study for nine weeks | Teaching for nine weeks |

This plan had several characteristics which may be mentioned. (a) Every student had at least one period of study after a period of practice. This was considered to be very desirable. One half of the students had two periods of study following periods of practice. Under the semester plan, one half of the students do practice teaching the first eighteen weeks, and the other half the last eighteen weeks; thus the second group has no period of study following their student teaching. Morrison's plan gave both groups periods of study after periods of teaching. (b) The two sections were selected on the basis of ability as judged by the faculty. The poorer section had two periods of student teaching, each following a period of study. The first period of study for this group gave the faculty an

[5] *Ibid.*, p. 197.
[6] *Ibid.*, p. 200.
[7] *Ibid.*, p. 206.

opportunity to do whatever was necessary to remedy any weaknesses which they thought existed in these students. Then, after nine weeks of teaching, the faculty had another period of nine weeks devoted to remedying weaknesses revealed in the period of teaching. This was followed by a further nine-week period of teaching which enabled students to gain experience based upon the instruction given them in their second nine weeks of study. This group was held out of teaching at the beginning of the year until they had had an additional nine weeks of maturing. By having student teaching during the second nine weeks, they had the advantage of one period of study after teaching, which they would not have had under the semester plan. (c) Although there was a gap of nine weeks between the first and the second period of student teaching, twenty-four weeks elapsed in the case of every student between the beginning and the end of his period of student teaching.

Morrison's revised program was put into effect immediately in both state normal schools. The curricula in the two schools were substantially the same. The curriculum, as organized and put into operation at Keene, serves as the basis for this discussion. The two-year general curriculum for elementary-school teachers is chosen for purposes of illustration.[8] The curriculum shows clearly the principles enunciated in Morrison's program. The following is the organization of the new curriculum as it appeared in 1919-1920, after it had been in operation for about two years:

TWO-YEAR GENERAL CURRICULUM FOR ELEMENTARY-SCHOOL TEACHERS[9]

FIRST YEAR

	Semester Hours	
	First	Second
Field and Course	Semester	Semester
Professional Study		
Education	3	3
Observation	2	2
Methodological		
Reading, Spelling, Language, Penmanship, Physiology and Hygiene, Geography, Plays and Games, Arithmetic, Literature and Grammar, History and Civics	10	10

[8] *Catalog and Circular of Information of the New Hampshire State Normal School at Keene*, pp. 24-25. 1919-1920.

[9] *Ibid.*, pp. 24-25.

Academic and Methodological
    Drawing, Music, Manual Arts, Domestic Arts, Nature
        Study and Gardening........................   11   11

                                              26   26

SECOND YEAR

Professional Study
    Education..   3
    Observation......................................   2
    Sociology..   2
    School Law......................................   1

Professional Experience and Concurrent Professional Study
    Practice Teaching (daily, full-time, for eighteen weeks)
    and School Management (weekly conferences with super-
    visor)...   20

Methodological
    Plays and Games................................   1

Academic and Methodological
    Drawing...   5
    Music...   2
    Manual Arts.....................................   4
    Domestic Arts...................................   4
    Nature Study and Gardening.....................   4

                                               28   20

SOME FUNDAMENTAL PRINCIPLES OF THE NEW PROGRAM

The principles of Morrison's plan are clearly in operation in this curriculum. An examination of the catalog of the normal school confirms the practice of alternating the study of theory with experience in the training school. It says:

> For greater efficiency the senior year is divided into quarters; half the class study program during the first and third quarters, while the other half is practicing and reversing the work for the second and fourth quarters.[10]

The evidence is clear that there was a very close relationship between the courses in education and the work of the training school. The relationship of the work in education in the first year to experience in the training school is brought out in a statement in the catalog which says that:

> During the first year each student spends one hour of each week in the grade schools, observing specially assigned lessons in various subjects. This observation, however, is followed by an hour helping grade pupils individ-

[10] *Ibid.*, p. 25.

ually or in small groups. These two hours familiarize the students with the atmosphere of the schoolroom and are a most desirable preparation for the practice work with classes during the second year. The observation forms the basis of class work in the first recitation of the following day.[11]

This statement indicates the general nature of the work in education in the first year. Several items are worthy of note. (*a*) Clearly students went into the training school for active participation at the beginning of their work in the normal school. (*b*) They continued this work throughout the first year as active room assistants. (*c*) They did considerable teaching of individual pupils and small groups. (*d*) In the second year they had alternate nine-week periods of study and full-time responsible student teaching. (*e*) It is clear that the work in education in the first year was based to a very large degree on the experience of two hours a week in the training school.

This curriculum represented several innovations which contributed noteworthy values in teacher education and which may be mentioned at this point in summary.

1. Theory and practice were made as nearly simultaneous as possible by the plan of alternation of teaching and study in the second year.

2. A direct, immediate, and high-level attack upon the professional study of teaching in the elementary schools was made possible by the omission of the deadening reviews previously found in the curricula of the normal schools of the state.

3. Methodology of elementary-school and junior-high-school subjects was learned by normal-school students through a direct approach to the materials of those subjects and their organization for purposes of pupil-education without previous academic study, i.e., a direct approach to the study of the professional organization of materials for teaching purposes and the almost simultaneous use of those materials in actual teaching. This may be called the methodological study of subject matter. It was carried on in the closest connection with experience and at all times related to that experience.

This plan was inaugurated at both Plymouth and Keene in the fall of 1916.[12] It has been in operation at both schools since that time without a great amount of modification except that the curricula have been extended in length and other curricula have been added. In principle the plan of teacher education has remained sub-

[11] *Ibid.*, p. 32.
[12] Morrison, Henry C. "Reorganization of Program of the Normal Schools." *Report of the Superintendent of Public Instruction*, p. 203. 1916.

stantially as established at that time. All the curricula of both normal schools are now organized under these principles.

FUNDAMENTAL CONCEPTIONS UNDERLYING NEW NORMAL-SCHOOL CURRICULUM

Morrison's conception of the normal-school curriculum was expressed several years later in a discussion which throws a good deal of light on this new curriculum. He had worked his ideas out in New Hampshire. He now discussed some aspects of the theory involved.[13] Some features of his discussion represent fundamental considerations which have considerable significance. Under the philosophy which Morrison had formulated, the preparation of a teacher had four important aspects:

1. The first element in teacher preparation was adequate academic scholarship.[14] Morrison had concluded, however, that four years of properly organized high-school study ought to give a teacher adequate academic preparation for teaching in the lower grades without the reviews commonly found in normal school curricula. He expressed the whole matter in these words:

. . . The bane of many schools, to put it bluntly, is in the fact that people who assume to teach, even in the elementary school, do not know enough. Many normal schools are keenly conscious of the fact and devote so much of their limited time to reviews of academic work that they have no time left for professional preparation proper. The bona fide graduate of a reputable secondary school ought to know enough to teach in elementary grades. The difficulty in fact seems to be that some normal schools are willing to accept secondary school graduates whose principals would never venture to grant a college entrance certificate, and in turn to pass along such students into the teaching profession. A further difficulty is often found in the fact that thoroughly good high-school graduates have often never studied at all the sciences and history and literature which are so peculiarly a necessity to the young person who is destined to meet the inquisitive minds of children in the elementary grades.[15]

Morrison's further suggestion that normal schools should not accept some of the personally weak material which comes to them, and also his thought that certain specified high-school subjects of a preprofessional nature should be required in the case of students who plan to attend normal school, were fundamental considerations.[16] He concluded by stating that:

[13] Morrison, Henry C. "What Training Does the Superintendent Need in his Elementary Teachers?" *Elementary School Journal*, 22: 347-351. January, 1920.
[14] *Ibid.*, p. 348.　　　[15] *Ibid.*, p. 348.　　　[16] *Ibid.*, p. 348.

. . . It is plainly essential that normal schools should be able to limit their academic courses to those which are mainly methodological in character.[17]

2. The second essential element in the preparation of an elementary-school teacher as conceived by Morrison was an understanding of the educative process.[18] This, it was said, was not intended to be a philosophy of education. Morrison held that the young elementary-school teacher

. . . can find an insight into a notion of education as a process of growth in the individual, sufficient to make her capable of intelligent discrimination between what is education for the elementary pupil and what is not—enough, let us say, to enable her to picture to herself what the elementary school is or ought to be trying to do. Modern biology and psychology provide an abundance of data for such a course.[19]

3. The third aspect of the preparation of an elementary-school teacher according to Morrison's theory of teacher education consisted of what he called the educational technology of the teaching field for which the teacher was prepared.[20] He postulated that:

Intelligent understanding is pretty apt to breed conscientiousness. Lack of understanding spells apathy.[21]

All such problems as child welfare, child health, safety education, and similar aspects of the work of the school which are often placed under the supervision of some one other than the teacher "find the understanding teacher their most effective aid."[22] On the other hand the teacher who does not understand is "an irritating stumbling block."[23] Morrison thought of these things as extra-curricular activities of a very necessary kind with which teachers must be equipped to deal intelligently.

The fundamental nature of the kind of study of education on which Morrison placed a great deal of stress is well expressed in his statement that:

. . . The school is the place in which all the child-welfare roads cross. The teacher is in a position to know sooner than most people when children begin to need public protection. If she is intelligent and keen about the matter, she is very likely to be able to prevent a world of suffering and crime; if she is ignorant of the whole matter, she is commonly apathetic, not only to the detriment of the school itself, but also to the sacrifice of one of the school's most conspicuous opportunities.[24]

[17] *Ibid.*, p. 348.   [18] *Ibid.*, p. 348.   [19] *Ibid.*, p. 348.   [20] *Ibid.*, p. 345.
[21] *Ibid.*, p. 345.   [22] *Ibid.*, p. 345.   [23] *Ibid.*, p. 345.   [24] *Ibid.*, p. 350.

4. The fourth element in a professionally prepared teacher under Morrison's conception was an understanding of the theory and principles of teaching, called methodology, and ability and skill in the technique of teaching. It was these qualities that distinguished the intelligent teacher from the routinist—the teacher who understands why he does what he does and who bases his procedure upon a theory which serves as his guide in practice. Morrison distinguished clearly between (a) the theory and principles of teaching which he called methodology and (b) the technique of teaching. This is his statement:

Methodology is one thing and technique is quite another. Without the first the teacher becomes an unintelligent routinist; without the second she cannot teach. The young woman who comes to her task in a given grade with the best possible knowledge of the principles which govern effective and economical teaching in that grade will still have to learn how to teach unless she has learned the technique of teaching by practice in teaching. We must not be surprised if the superintendent is not impressed by the scientific equipment of the methodologist who can not teach.[25]

Even at the time at which Morrison wrote, a growing body of well-founded principles of teaching was available as a basis for courses in normal schools. He put emphasis on this aspect of the teacher's preparation as well as on the place and function of student teaching as the only means of acquiring an effective technique of teaching. He summed up the idea in these words:

Here is of course the point at which . . . the professional school either succeeds or fails, for here it is that the student in training either learns to teach or does not learn. The plea that the normal school does not wish to teach any particular method, but only the "great fundamentals" will no longer hold. Time was when it would. That was the day of the widely exploited empirical devices for teaching reading or arithmetic or what not. We have in the place of that empiricism today, a body of principles scientifically determined which gives us a generalized basis for the methodology of most of the schoolroom arts. . . . In effect the normal school has for most of the subjects of elementary schools a teachable methodology.[26]

All this, as described, was what Morrison meant by "pedagogy." Four elements in his theory of teacher education stood out prominently: (a) an elementary-school teacher who was superior as a person and who had acquired in the secondary school a general academic background adequate to enable the normal school to devote all its energies to professional preparation from the outset;

[25] Ibid., p. 351. [26] Ibid., pp. 350-351.

(*b*) a teacher made intelligent concerning the larger social problems related to child welfare and development by certain broadly conceived courses concerned chiefly with social case studies of unadjusted children and similar fields; (*c*) a teacher who possessed an understanding of the theory and principles of teaching which served as a guide to intelligent practice; (*d*) a teacher who was able to teach effectively in terms of his or her theory.

Thus the elementary-school teacher was conceived as a person who had in very broad relationships a basic professional understanding of the child whom he or she taught and whose technique of teaching was soundly grounded in an understanding of basic theory and principles comparable to those of workers in other professions. Such a teacher knew the reasons for the procedures which were used, was skillful in technique, and keenly sensitive to child welfare.

All these considerations were basic in the normal-school curriculum established by Morrison in 1916 in New Hampshire. This curriculum was notable at that time in these respects: (*a*) the absence of academic study, especially reviews, and the direct methodological approach in professional study of elementary school subjects; (*b*) the breadth and quality of the professional preparation given under the titles of psychology, pedagogy, and educational sociology; (*c*) the dependence upon student teaching and other forms of participation as a basis for acquiring the technique of teaching, including the use of subject matter in teaching.

The aim was to produce a teacher who was intelligent in broad zones related to children and the function of schools and other institutions of society which dealt with children from a custodial or a welfare point of view, and one who also possesesd a skillful classroom technique based upon a definite theory of teaching.

OUTLINE OF THE NEW THREE-YEAR CURRICULA

The two-year curriculum established under Morrison's reorganization continued without material change for a decade and a half. Various phases of it, of course, evolved. The extensive laboratory-school facilities which are described in another chapter were developed. This made possible a better operation of the curriculum from year to year. This curriculum finally developed, in 1933, into a three-year curriculum,[27] the form of which is presented here:

[27] Since this chapter was written, it has become a four-year curriculum.

Three-Year Curriculum for Elementary-School Teachers[28]

For Teachers of the First Six Grades and Rural Schools

FIRST YEAR

| | Semester Hours | |
| | First Semester | Second Semester |
Field and Course		
Education		
Introduction to Teaching and Educational Psychology	2	
Educational Psychology		3
English		
Oral and Written English	3	2
Handwriting		1
Social Science		
American History Background	3	
Geography		3
Natural Science		
Nature	2	2
Art		
Art Activities and Appreciation	2	2
Mathematics		
General Mathematics		3
Music		
Music in the Elementary School	2	2
Health and Physical Education		
Personal Hygiene	2	
Physical Education	1	1
Orientation		
Library Usage and Social Customs	1	1
	18	20

SECOND YEAR

| | Semester Hours | |
| | First Semester | Second Semester |
Field and Course		
Education		
Observation and Conferences	1	
Observation and Preliminary Participation		1
Educational Sociology		3
English		
Children's Literature and Reading	3	3

[28] New Hampshire Normal Schools. *Circular of Information.* "Program of Studies: Curricula and Courses," p. 7. 1933.

Social Science
    American History and Citizenship..................   3   3
    Geography.......................................   3

Natural Science
    Biology..   3

Industrial Arts
    Industrial Arts..................................   2   2

Music
    Music Appreciation..............................   3

Mathematics
    Arithmetic......................................   3   3

Health and Physical Education
    Physical Education..............................   1   1
                                    ——   ——
                                   19   19

THIRD YEAR

Field and Course	Semester Hours First Semester	Second Semester
Education		
School Law, Professional Ethics and Program of Studies	2	
Principles of Elementary Education.................		2
Rural Schools.....................................		2
Student Teaching.................................		16
English		
Literature.......................................	3	
Social Science		
Economics.......................................	3	
Geography.......................................	3	
New Hampshire Resources........................	1	
Natural Science		
General Science..................................	3	
Art		
Art Activities and Appreciation...................	3	
Health and Physical Education		
Health Education.................................	2	
	—	—
	20	20

CONCLUSION

These developments in the preparation of elementary-school teachers have continued down to the present time. The normal schools have satisfied the test of experience in the state. They have popular favor. So far as the consensus of judgment of those who have had extended experience with these procedures is concerned, they have justified themselves. The graduates of the state normal schools who have been prepared under this plan meet the approval of superintendents who have occasion to employ graduates of many normal schools, to a greater extent than do those prepared in other teacher-education institutions.[29] The basis for determining teaching merit which was used is the subject of critical comment at a later point in this study.

[29] Butterfield, E. W. "Normal Schools." *Report of the State Board of Education*, pp. 135-154. Concord, New Hampshire: State Board of Education. 1930.

CHAPTER VI

BEGINNINGS IN THE ESTABLISHMENT OF POLICIES FOR THE EDUCATION AND PROFESSIONAL PREPARATION OF SECONDARY-SCHOOL TEACHERS

SHORTLY after his appointment as state superintendent of public instruction, Morrison began a campaign of personal inspection of secondary schools. He spent the larger part of his time in the field among the schools. He considered his work to be that of superintendent.[1] He personally made extended field-studies of the teaching in the secondary schools of the state. In 1913, under a new law, three assistant state superintendents of public instruction were added to the state education department. Two of them under their assignments in the organization which Morrison established immediately began, under his direction, an intensive field-study of the secondary schools of the state with comprehensive written reports which amounted almost to surveys. One devoted himself largely to industrial arts, home economics, commerce, and agriculture. These courses had developed rapidly in the high schools. The second assistant state superintendent gave special attention to the state normal schools and to general work in the secondary schools, as well as considerable attention to elementary schools. The third had charge of the office of the state department of education at Concord. The two deputy superintendents in their field-studies accumulated a large amount of factual material about the secondary schools.

These field-studies early revealed the fact that secondary-school teachers generally had a good academic education as judged by the standards of those days, but were almost totally without professional preparation.[2] Morrison did not, however, give major attention to the preparation of secondary-school teachers in his earliest reports.

[1] Morrison, Henry C. "Inspecting Schools" and "Lectures of the Superintendent." *Report of the Superintendent of Public Instruction*, pp. 15-18. 1906.
[2] Morrison, Henry C. *Report of the Superintendent of Public Instruction*, pp. 332-333. 1908.

He had problems connected with the development of a more satisfactory staff for elementary schools, the question of child labor, and the extension of professional supervision, which seemed at that time to overshadow in importance a good many other needs. They required his major attention.

TRANSIENCY OF SECONDARY-SCHOOL TEACHERS

The transient character of the secondary teaching staff, as revealed in the factual studies of the teaching personnel, appeared to Morrison to be a particularly distressing feature of the secondary-school situation in New Hampshire. Given reasonably good teachers, he regarded permanency in the teaching staff as a prime requisite of efficiency in the public elementary- and secondary-schools of the state. In his first biennial report he commented on the transient condition of the teaching staff. More than one-third of all the secondary teachers had been in service less than a year; three-fourths had been appointed in the preceding five years. Only eighteen out of seventy principals had been in service more than five years. Investigation revealed that these conditions were normal and not peculiar to that year. It appeared that one-third or more of the secondary-school staff had been for a long time new to the state every year.[3] The fact of such a highly transient secondary-school teaching staff was deemed to be one of the most powerful influences in limiting the real effects of genuine secondary education. Instead of producing in the population those desirable results which were supposed to come from attendance at high schools and academies, high-school teaching degenerated into lesson-hearing from textbooks, conducted by young college graduates who lacked professional preparation and who changed to other positions every year or two. Morrison concluded that in the secondary school there could be no adequate institutional life if that highly important institution was to continue to be in charge of a succession of immature young men just out of college who remained for only a brief period. He did note some improvements in the fact that high-school and academy principalships were less and less frequently stepping stones to other professions.[4]

Morrison's conviction concerning the desirability of reasonable

[3] Morrison, Henry C. *Report of the Superintendent of Public Instruction*, p. 188. 1906.
[4] *Ibid.*, pp. 188-189.

permanence in the teaching staff was expressed in vigorous language
and he later made the need for greater permanence and continuity
of service among secondary-school teachers one of the foundations
upon which he built his proposed program of teacher education in
the state.   In his first report he declared that after good character
and efficiency, there is perhaps nothing more important in the schoolroom than permanency in the teacher's chair.   As he conducted his
studies of the ever-changing teaching personnel, he was forced by
the facts he found to the conclusion that new teachers, new ways,
new acquaintanceships to be made by pupils and teacher resulted in
friction and ill-adjustment in a school, which was often prohibitive
of good, work and ruinously expensive in time lost both to pupils and
to the community.   He expressed the conviction that a moderately
good teacher of good character and of sufficient education, who remains at his or her post year after year, who knows the children and
parents, and who understands the community life is far to be pre-
ferred to the more able person who comes and goes and who by the
very fact of transiency leaves little permanent good effect on pupils.
Morrison believed that this transient teacher was little more of a
vital personality to the children than the actors in a drama would
be to older persons.[5]

TWO NOTABLE DISCUSSIONS OF THE PREPARATION OF SECONDARY-SCHOOL TEACHERS

Morrison's real attack upon the problem of preparation of secondary-school teachers began in 1912 and continued with unabated
vigor from that time to the close of his administration in 1917.
During that period policies designed to improve conditions which
scientific studies had revealed were discussed.   No special provision
was made in state normal schools in New Hampshire at that time
for the preparation of high-school teachers.   The report of 1914[6]
discussed the question thoroughly, and that of 1916[7] presented the
situation with great vigor.   These two reports are significant for
the discussions of the preparation of secondary-school teachers which
they contain and the effects which eventually grew out of them.
They set in motion influences which led to the steps finally taken to

[5] *Ibid.*, p. 188.

[6] Morrison, Henry C. "The Training of Teachers." *Report of the Superintendent of Public Instruction*, pp. 143-164.   1914.

[7] Morrison, Henry C. "The Education, Training and Character of the Teaching
Force." *Report of the Superintendent of Public Instruction*, pp. 171-193.   1916.

provide a staff of professionally prepared high-school teachers for the state.

Two things in particular seemed desirable to Morrison as a means of establishing permanence in the secondary-school teaching staff. The first was more men teachers. He had found that marriage was the great interrupter of continuity in the schoolroom. He knew that this would always be the case so long as the bulk of the teachers were young women. He declared with emphasis that a much greater proportion of strong and virile men is needed in the classrooms of secondary schools. He asserted that it would be impossible to have even a moderately permanent teaching force in the secondary school unless two-thirds to three-quarters of the teachers were men. He was also impressed by the fact that boys of high-school age need the influence of men in far greater measure than they get it. He reasoned that the conditions necessary to secure more men in secondary-school teaching were better salaries, more assurance of protection in service, and provision for old age.[8]

PROPOSAL OF A COLLEGE OF EDUCATION

Morrison was approaching the source of the difficulty with the teaching staff of the secondary school when he pointed out that so long as nine-tenths of the secondary-school teachers of the state were drawn from other states, just so long would New Hampshire be a mere training ground for teachers who remained in the state only until they could get calls to other states. The field-studies revealed a tendency for the weaker and less efficient to remain in the state. In discussing this problem Morrison stated his often-repeated principle that in the long run every section of the state must raise, educate, and train as many elementary-school teachers as it needs. His data contained convincing evidence that the state as a whole must raise, educate, and train as many superintendents and secondary-school teachers as it needs. He concluded, therefore, that a college of education in the state would do much to solve this question of permanency in the teaching force.

In the later years of his administration, after the two deputy superintendents had completed a number of field-studies, the situation with reference to the teaching personnel of the secondary school seemed to Morrison to be critical. The same faults were found

[8] Morrison, Henry C. "Need of a More Permanent Force." *Report of the Superintendent of Public Instruction*, p. 161. 1914.

which he had discussed in earlier reports. In the 1914 report he expressed the matter emphatically and stressed again the two great faults, namely, lack of professional preparation and brevity of service. These facts, he repeated, pointed to the need of a school of collegiate grade for the professional preparation of New Hampshire young people to teach in the schools of New Hampshire. After making the foregoing statement Morrison continued by saying that the percentage of teachers who were thoroughly well grounded in the subjects which they taught was much lower than four years of collegiate study could justify. He said, however, that the need was not more study but better study and better teaching on the part of college faculties. He discovered that it was an uncommon experience to find a high-school teacher who had any adequate conception of teaching as teaching. The main reason was that the young college graduate came to his task with little or no previous professional study and with a conception of teaching derived from the college classroom which, the field-studies seemed clearly to reveal, was certainly very much out of place with young people of high-school age. As a result inefficiency followed as inevitably it must. Some young teachers were found, of course, who had pedagogical ingenuity and address. They succeeded well in the beginning. Others learned to teach by experience, but with a teaching force of which one-third was new every year not much could be expected from the lessons of experience. Very many tended to become formalists and wore themselves out year after year in attempting to accomplish the impossible.

In spite of these evident facts Morrison discovered that many teachers in the high schools and academies of the state were earnestly conscious of their own limitations as teachers and were trying their best to improve themselves by private study. A large number attended the winter high-school institutes. A minority still felt a sense of superiority and looked with indulgence tinctured with contempt upon suggestions for self-improvement. There were many individual instances in which high-school teachers had developed a good professional spirit and had shown marked improvement in professional capacity. Morrison again concluded his discussion by a reiteration of the need for a four-year college course for every secondary teacher, with professional study emphasized in every year.[9]

[9] Morrison, Henry C. "Need of Higher Training for Secondary Teachers and Superintendents." *Report of Superintendent of Public Instruction*, pp. 159-160. 1914.

Clearly his conception of the preparation of secondary-school teachers was not one in which two years of professional work is superimposed upon two years of purely academic liberal-arts study. Morrison's conception included a four-year curriculum, professionalized from the first year to the last. That, however, did not preclude the cultural education of the teacher as a part of his professional education.

In his last biennial report, written in 1916, after several years of extended field studies of secondary schools by two assistant state superintendents and to some extent by himself, Morrison used even more vigorous language than ever before in summarizing the facts concerning the lack of preparation of secondary-school teachers. He said:

We have less than a dozen teachers of modern languages in the state who are thoroughly competent in education to teach modern languages in a high school, but most of the remainder are passably competent. Less than twenty who are thoroughly competent for mathematics; a very few for Latin; almost nobody in English, unless the pedantic conception of the language and literature of the mother tongue which most of them bring from college is competency.[10]

Again in the 1916 report, Morrison described in vigorous language the instability, the immaturity, the inexperience, and the lack of professional understanding and ability which had been found in the secondary-school teaching staff. He said:

We have still in this state, as in most states, a secondary teaching staff which is wholly untrained. Not one per cent of the secondary teachers of the state have ever had any professional training at all comparable to what forty-four per cent of the elementary teaching force has had. A few have taken courses in education in college and that is a help.

He continued by saying that:

you turn over your boys and girls at their most impressionable age to striplings who are without training or experience, who have no notions of teaching except those which they bring with them from college; and who in most cases have no intention whatever of teaching beyond the few years which form a fitting interlude between college and matrimony. We would not deny them the latter, but we do think that if they are going to teach at all they ought to learn how to teach, just as do the girls who are two years younger and who are teaching in the elementary schools.

Our notebooks and records of inspection tell a wretched tale of the farcical instruction commonly found in the classrooms of these young teachers—

[10] Morrison, Henry C. "The Education, Training and Character of the Teaching Force." *Report of the Superintendent of Public Instruction*, p. 188. 1916.

particularly in English, both language and literature, in history, in languages and in science. Ordinarily teaching consists in assigning pages out of an incomprehensible textbook or dictating from a college notebook. And this to boys and girls of an age which needs skillful teaching beyond any age other than that of the primary school.[11]

This is strong language, but it undoubtedly correctly depicts the situation. Ample records in the form of extensive field-studies of secondary schools furnished sufficient documentation for these statements. They truly describe conditions which existed in New Hampshire high schools at that time as well as in the high schools of many other states.

The studies of the sources and preparation of secondary-school teachers contained in the biennial report of 1914-1916 indicated the colleges from which the secondary-school teachers of the state came. The place of graduation of every secondary-school teacher was located. It appeared that the state drew its high-school academic teachers from sixty-three different institutions, some of which were located in distant parts of the country. Morrison commented on this fact. He felt that it furnished evidence that New Hampshire did not secure the best personal material. Other things being equal, he said, the best of every graduating class easily find positions near home. It was of course true that some superior teachers would come from distant places, but as a general rule it was inevitable that the majority should be composed of those who, finding themselves without places near their colleges, located in those states which were failing to graduate from colleges as many teachers as were needed annually to fill the vacancies in their own secondary schools. These facts seemed to account in part for the very unstable teaching force, with two-fifths of all the secondary teachers new to their places each year. This situation was almost fatal to the efficiency of the state's secondary schools. It was a fact that only about 9 per cent of the whole secondary teaching force had been graduated from New Hampshire institutions. The number who were born in New Hampshire and had been graduated from colleges outside of the state was negligible. Morrison declared that:

. . . the remaining ninety-one per cent have no stake in New Hampshire, they are not personally the best of material, they do not understand our ways, and naturally they move at the first opportunity.[12]

[11] *Ibid.*, pp. 191-192.
[12] *Ibid.*, pp. 183-184.

NORMAL SCHOOLS NOT SUITABLE FOR PREPARATION OF
SECONDARY-SCHOOL TEACHERS

Morrison took strong ground against the preparation of secondary-school teachers in the state normal schools. He felt that the normal schools had enough and more than enough to do in the training of teachers for the elementary schools. He believed, also, that teachers in secondary schools needed four years of academic as well as professional preparation. They also needed the ripening process which would come from four years of study. At that time the existing normal schools in New Hampshire were two-year institutions. They had only recently required high-school graduation for admission. They devoted themselves strictly to professional preparation. The academic education of high-school teachers would require an academic faculty which the normal schools did not have at that time. The general advantages at the normal schools would be so lacking that they would attract only an inadequate enrollment of inferior material.[13] Undoubtedly this reasoning represented at the time a sound view of this particular problem in teacher education. The normal schools were falling far short of supplying the number of elementary-school teachers which the state needed. There was no prospect that they could meet that need for at least a decade or even longer. They had neither the faculties nor the equipment to give the proper education and professional preparation to secondary-school teachers.

ELEMENTS IN THE PREPARATION OF SECONDARY-
SCHOOL TEACHERS

The three main elements in the preparation of secondary-school teachers, in addition to the graduate preparation of superintendents, were set forth in Morrison's proposal. He said that a school of education at the state college should provide:

(1) For the general education of collegiate grade of young people who expect to teach in our secondary schools.
(2) For special academic preparation of such students for the specialties which they proposed to teach.
(3) For four years of special educational and pedagogical training; with practice teaching in some nearby high school. Dover, Newmarket, Rochester, Exeter, Somersworth, and Portsmouth ought to furnish ample ground for

[13] *Ibid.,* pp. 163-164.

such training. It would be desirable to establish a model small high school in Durham itself.

(4) For postgraduate work in education for prospective superintendents.[14]

KIND OF SCHOOL OF EDUCATION NEEDED

Morrison had great contempt for mere bookish preparation of teachers, but, on the other hand, the preparation which consisted of experience only seemed equally undesirable. He desired a fundamental preparation for secondary-school teachers based upon the serious study of psychology and education. He set forth some of the things which he believed a school of education should and should not do when he wrote the following:

> In the first place, it should not be a place in which instructors with a mere book knowledge of education may air that knowledge. Schools of education of that type are not uncommon. We find in such institutions, not infrequently, a young man all but wholly innocent of any actual teaching experience engaged in trying to teach young people how to teach "out of a book."
>
> In the second place, it should be a school in which the theory of education is closely and intimately tied up with the art and practice of teaching. Schools of education are not difficult to find in which in the school itself every principle which the school endeavors to inculcate is daily and hourly violated in its own practice.
>
> On the other hand, its instructors should be men of recognized standing in the field of education and psychology. The mistake should not be made of attempting to be "practical" by the device of simply calling in some successful high-school teacher as professor of education. This has at times been done.
>
> So far as possible the school of education should be related to our general state school system in much the same manner as the normal schools.[15]

PREPARATION OF SECONDARY-SCHOOL TEACHERS FOR THE SPECIAL SUBJECTS

The problem of securing secondary-school teachers for the special subjects such as home economics (called domestic arts at that time), industrial arts (called mechanic arts), and commerce was of serious concern in 1916. These subjects under Morrison's secondary-school policy were then developing rapidly in the high schools and academies of the state. They did not consist of a few courses which were permitted to be chosen as electives in some general curriculum. On the contrary, four-year curricula in home economics, industrial arts, commerce, agriculture, with each of these subjects

[14] *Ibid.*, p. 162.
[15] *Ibid.*, p. 163.

studied in well-organized sequences of courses for four years as the main field in the curriculum, had been established in large numbers in the state. Few suitable teachers, however, were available. This work, which Morrison regarded as exceedingly important, suffered for lack of effective teaching. It was necessary to allow teachers of superficial education, albeit some skill, to teach these subjects. Such teachers were found to be generally quite unsatisfactory. They lacked the cultural background which high-school teachers were thought to need. They were not capable of teaching outside of the mere skill aspects of their subjects. The desirable type of preparation for these special secondary-school teachers was discussed in the 1916 report. The kind of preparation which a school of education in a state like New Hampshire ought to offer, according to Morrison's conception, was described in considerable detail. He stressed the need for advanced study of the subjects in question and especially emphasized study of the applied sciences which are basic in these fields.

Concerning the current preparation of teachers for work in home economics in secondary schools and desirable preparation, Morrison had this to say:

> In domestic arts we are still drawing our teachers largely from the normal schools, though there is a goodly number of college graduates among them. Graduates of normal schools have not the education essential to adequate instruction in this curriculum in the secondary school. And, in truth, the graduates of colleges are prone to have had special training only of elementary and secondary grade—a smattering of cooking and sewing, a course in textiles, another in dietetics of doubtful scientific validity, and a vague round of household management. Now that girls are beginning to offer household arts as a college entrance unit, it ought to be and is practicable to train prospective teachers of household arts in applied physics, chemistry, and biology, in the advanced study of foods, fabrics, and house construction and sanitation, and in domestic economics properly considered. The college course for teachers ought very probably to be distinct from the general course in household arts.[16]

Morrison presented an extended discussion of the preparation of teachers for the so-called special subjects. He was greatly interested in those subjects and had a deep appreciation of their value in secondary education. He was concerned about the farcical teaching of many of the superficially prepared teachers of these subjects. He could see that genuine secondary education, with the emphasis

[16] *Ibid.,* p. 189.

on education as distinct from training, could not be gained under such teachers. The same principle was applied to industrial arts, concerning which Morrison said:

A four-years intensive course for teachers at the state college is needed, including advanced shop work in wood and metals, shop mathematics, applied physics and chemistry, the principles of machine construction, including the elements of steam, gas, and electrical engine design, and metallurgy. Such a teachers' course would utilize the same instructors and the same equipment as do the engineering courses, but it would be a distinct course directed to the end of preparation for teaching.[17]

Morrison's comment concerning the study of commerce in the secondary schools needs to be considered at length. It reveals his disapproval of a secondary-school curriculum which was limited quite exclusively to a somewhat narrow preparation in certain skills such as stenography, typewriting, bookkeeping, penmanship, and similar subjects. His discussion shows a conception of secondary education achieved through a study of commerce in its broader sense, and reveals an ideal of a commerce teacher who is a product of education in commerce as distinguished from mere training in a somewhat narrow range of technical commercial subjects. The broader conception appeared all through what Morrison wrote concerning the preparation of teachers for the special subjects, but it appeared particularly in what he said about the preparation of teachers for secondary-school work in commerce. This is what he wrote in 1916 concerning that subject:

Our commerce teachers as a class are distinctly the least educated, and there is no institution in sight prepared to give the necessary education. A few are well-educated college graduates who have prepared themselves by further study in a commercial school to teach stenography and typewriting and bookkeeping of a formalistic and unreal type. Of the remainder a few are graduates of normal schools which offer special courses in preparation for commerce teaching. The large majority are graduates of short courses in commercial schools. There are few if any in the state who are prepared to give instruction outside the field of stenography and typewriting and bookkeeping. In stenography and typewriting, while the course consumes an entirely unnecessary amount of time, the results are usually good. It is the intention of the department not to approve schools which allow this work to fall below an easily determined standard.

Secondary education in commerce cannot, however, be properly limited to stenography and typewriting, bookkeeping, and a futile course in penmanship. It ought to include the elements of commercial law, study of the ele-

[17] *Ibid.*, p. 189-190.

ments of political economy, of the banking and currency systems of this and the other principal commercial nations, and the conditions under which trade is carried on. The pupils ought also to be grounded in one or more of three modern languages—French, German and Spanish.

Much of the above is attempted but with scant results. Competent teachers are not available.

The position hardly admits of debate that a competent study of commerce ought to be one of the main elements in each of our city high-schools and in those of all the larger towns.

To meet the situation, it is proposed that four-year courses in commerce be established in the state college, particularly because they are needed for the training of teachers in our secondary schools, but also because our whole commercial life should be fortified by specific collegiate education of our future business men and women. The state college now ministers to a large part of the common life of the state, with its schools of agriculture, engineering in several branches, household arts, education, and the liberal arts which are and should be the setting of each of the practical arts. But it fails to reach one of the largest elements in our state life, to wit, commerce.[18]

PROFESSIONAL EDUCATION OF SUPERINTENDENTS

In addition to developing plans for the better education of elementary and secondary-school teachers the factual data which had accumulated indicated a clear need for a plan of teacher education which would provide educated and professionally prepared superintendents. The facts seemed to Morrison to point to the need for a small school for the professional preparation of superintendents to which a few selected people would be sent. He expressed this idea in the following language:

Another form of professional training which must sooner or later be provided, will be that of superintendents as such. True, the normal school of today furnishes an excellent training for the superintendent so far as it goes. It does not, however, furnish the necessary scope for the adequate training of a man who is a college graduate and a teacher of experience already. He needs a more vital and searching study, a more thoroughgoing discipline. Certainly the preliminary professional discipline of a man who is more than any other one responsible for the happiness, efficiency and citizenship of the whole rising generation of an entire community, ought to be no less than that of the physician or attorney or engineer. Possibly, we shall ultimately have a small training school for superintendents, under a very strong head, to which teachers will be sent by selection for further study and preparation when they shall have demonstrated that they have supervisory timber in them.[19]

[18] *Ibid.*, pp. 190-191.
[19] Morrison, Henry C. *Report of the Superintendent of Public Instruction*, p. 333. 1908.

Certain policies of teacher education developed in New Hampshire as an outcome of the vigorous attack upon the problem of professional preparation of secondary-school teachers which was carried on throughout Morrison's administration, but which culminated in the last four years of his period of service as state superintendent. These developments will be discussed in a later chapter.

REALIZATION OF IDEALS

The ideals for which Morrison struggled came to realization after 1919, but not precisely in the manner in which he hoped that his plans for the preparation of secondary-school teachers would be consummated. The state did not establish a school of education at the state college. It seemed desirable, therefore, to carry forward in the state normal schools a comprehensive program of teacher preparation for secondary schools. Before 1919 the normal schools had made a start in the preparation of teachers for junior high schools. A few years later that beginning developed into a fully organized plan for the preparation of secondary-school teachers.

CHAPTER VII

PROGRESS IN THE PREPARATION OF SECONDARY-SCHOOL TEACHERS

SHORTLY after 1900 the state normal school in New Hampshire began to offer advanced work beyond the traditional two-year curriculum. This was accomplished largely by adding what were then called postgraduate studies and by offering opportunities for college graduates to pursue professional studies. In 1905 Plymouth offered a one-year postgraduate curriculum leading to the degree of bachelor of pedagogy. Admission to this curriculum was granted to graduates of the two-year curriculum. A special one-year curriculum leading to a diploma was offered to college graduates. There is no evidence that anyone took the degree curriculum. It merely represented the earliest effort to extend the curriculum. A few college graduates took the one year of work as offered for such people and received diplomas. In 1910 a definite announcement of a three-year curriculum was made.[1] This was a curriculum for teachers and supervisors of music, art, and home economics (called domestic economy) in elementary and secondary schools.

BEGINNINGS IN PREPARATION OF SECONDARY-SCHOOL TEACHERS

That step may be regarded as the real beginning of the development from a two-year institution in the direction of teachers-college status. It may also be regarded as the real beginning of the plans for preparation of secondary-school teachers in New Hampshire normal schools.

The work of these new curricula followed somewhat closely that of the general curriculum. Some special study of the subject in which the student had chosen to specialize was allowed. The work was identical with that of the general curriculum for elementary-school teachers in the first year. It was the same in part in the second year. The third year was devoted to advanced study in the special subject and included student teaching in that subject. There is,

[1] *Forty-first Annual Catalog and Circular of the Plymouth Normal School,* p. 16. 1910-1912.

however, no evidence of any enrollment in these new curricula at the time that they were introduced.

The announcements of special provision for teachers who desired to specialize to some extent in music, art, and home economics continued to be made in the catalog at Plymouth after their first appearance. In 1916 an announcement of a three-year curriculum for junior-high-school teachers was made. Paragraphs were found in the catalogs announcing these extensions of the work of the institution. No actual curriculum, however, appeared in the catalog.[2] The list of graduates for June, 1915, included the names of seven students who received a special diploma for three years of work.[3] Thus it is apparent that a start had been made on three-year curricula which prepared students for doing some work in junior- and senior-high schools. The teachers of home economics, in particular, were employed for secondary-school positions.[4] This was the real beginning of actually providing teachers for secondary schools by the state normal schools. It took place before the end of the administration of Morrison as state superintendent. No evidence had appeared by that time which justified any hope that the state university might be depended upon for an adequate supply of professionally educated teachers for the high schools of the state.

About the same situation was found at the other state normal school at Keene,[5] which had been established in 1908. A third year appeared in the catalog for 1916-1917 and was called the junior-high year. There is no point in reviewing in more detail what was found at that school, since the two institutions were nearly identical in curriculum and procedure. What has been said concerning Plymouth holds in the main for Keene.

EARLY DEVELOPMENT OF CURRICULA FOR SECONDARY-SCHOOL TEACHERS

The development of curricula for the preparation of junior- and senior-high-school teachers went forward rapidly after the beginning had been made. In 1920-1921 the following curricula were offered in the two state normal schools:

[2] "Curriculum for Teachers of Special Subjects" and "Junior High School Courses," *Catalog of Plymouth Normal School, New Hampshire,* p. 31. 1916.

[3] *Ibid.,* p. 51.

[4] Morrison, Henry C. "The Education, Training and Character of Our Teaching Force." *Report of the Superintendent of Public Instruction,* p. 189. 1916.

[5] *Catalog and Circular of Information of the New Hampshire State Normal School at Keene,* p. 24. 1916-1917.

1. Three-year curriculum for junior-high-school and senior-high-school teachers with some modification in the first two years and the addition of a year to the two-year curriculum (Plymouth and Keene).
2. Three-year curriculum for teachers of home economics in junior-high schools and senior-high schools (Plymouth and Keene).
3. Three-year curriculum for teachers of commerce in senior-high schools (Plymouth and Keene).
4. Three-year curriculum for teachers and supervisors of music (Keene).
5. Three-year curriculum for teachers and supervisors of art (Keene).[6]

These curricula represented the beginnings of what Morrison had recommended to be done at the state university in teacher preparation. The catalogs of the state normal schools at this time did not show extended offerings of courses in the subjects with which the curricula dealt. The courses in education included a semester course in adolescent psychology, a course of similar length in secondary education, and another in problems of the secondary schools. A year's work appeared in the catalog in Latin, French, and Spanish. Stenography, typewriting, office practice and appliances, business correspondence, spelling, penmanship, commercial arithmetic, and bookkeeping represented the additions in commerce.[7] Corresponding extensions were made in other fields. The richly cultural and educational work which Morrison had recommended had not yet come. On the other hand, a promising beginning had been made with slender resources. It was the best that could be done under the circumstances.

E. W. Butterfield had become state superintendent of public instruction in 1917, and he had begun immediately to develop a new normal-school program built upon Morrison's foundation but projected another decade into the future. He early postulated the futility of the expectation that any but institutions completely under the jurisdiction of the state board of education and devoted primarily

[6] *Catalog of the New Hampshire State Normal School at Plymouth*, pp. 27-30. 1921; and *Catalog and Circular of Information of the New Hampshire State Normal School at Keene*, pp. 20-26. 1920-21.

[7] "Commerce." *Catalog and Circular of Information of the New Hampshire State Normal School at Keene*, pp. 42-44. 1920.

and exclusively to teacher preparation could ever be depended upon as the instruments of the state in placing all schools in the hands of educated and professionally prepared teachers. He proceeded to build in the light of this postulate. He had had a prominent part in the field-studies made during Morrison's régime and he based his conclusions in part on these results.

A DECADE OF PROGRESS IN THE PREPARATION OF SECONDARY-SCHOOL TEACHERS

After the beginning which was made between 1908 and 1920 in the preparation of teachers for secondary schools, progress was rapid. What took place in the next ten years in extending the preparation of secondary-school teachers is indicated by listing the curricula as they were found in 1933. They were as follows:[8]

1. Three-year curriculum for junior-high-school teachers of both general and special subjects (Plymouth and Keene).
2. Three-year curriculum for supervisors: (a) of art; (b) of music; and (c) of art and music, in elementary and secondary schools (Plymouth and Keene).
3. Four-year curriculum for high-school teachers of commerce and other subjects (Plymouth).
4. Four-year curriculum for high-school teachers of English and other subjects (Keene).
5. Four-year curriculum for high-school teachers of history and other subjects (Plymouth).
6. Four-year curriculum for teachers of home economics and other subjects in junior- and senior-high schools (Keene).
7. Four-year curriculum in trade and industry for teachers of shop and related subjects in junior- and senior-high schools (Keene).

In these developments is seen the attainment of teachers-college status. The adoption of these curricula and their effective operation in the normal schools, with a substantial enrollment in each curriculum, was a beginning of the consummation of Morrison's ideal for the preparation of secondary-school teachers in the state.

Typical three-year and four-year curricula are shown in the following pages.

[8] New Hampshire Normal Schools. *Circular of Information.* "Program of Studies: Curricula and Courses," pp. 3-5. 1933.

THREE-YEAR CURRICULUM FOR JUNIOR-HIGH-SCHOOL TEACHERS AND TEACHERS OF SPECIAL SUBJECTS[9]

FIRST YEAR

Field and Course	Semester Hours First Semester	Second Semester
Education		
Introduction to Teaching	3	
Educational Psychology		3
English		
Current Literature	3	
Composition and Rhetoric		3
Penmanship	(1)0	
Expression		(1)0
Social Science		
History and Civilization	3	3
Natural Science		
General Science	3	3
Mathematics		
Junior-High-School Mathematics	3	3
Health and Physical Education		
Physical Education	1	1
Orientation		
Personal Hygiene and Social Customs		(1)0
Electives	3	3
	19	19

SECOND YEAR

Field and Course	Semester Hours First Semester	Second Semester
Education		
Secondary Education: Organization and Administration of Secondary Schools with Especial Reference to New Hampshire	3	
Educational Sociology (Especially related to New Hampshire conditions)		3
English		
Essay and Short Story	3	
Public Speaking and Debate		3

[9] *Ibid.*, pp. 8-13.

Field and Course	Semester Hours First Semester	Second Semester
Social Science		
Modern European History	3	3
General Sociology	3	
Natural Science		
Biology	3	3
Health and Physical Education		
Physical Education	1	1
Electives	3	6
	19	19

THIRD YEAR

Field and Course	Semester Hours First Semester	Second Semester
Education		
Principles of Teaching in Secondary Schools	3	
History and Organization of New Hampshire Education		1
New Hampshire School Law and Code of Ethics		1
Current Educational Problems		1
Student Teaching		16
English		
Diagnostic and Remedial Treatment for Individual Difficulties in English	3	
Social Science		
Economics	3	
Geography in the Junior-High School	3	
United States History and Civil Government	3	
Health and Physical Education		
Physical Education	1	
Electives	3	
	19	19

REQUIREMENTS GOVERNING CHOICE OF ELECTIVES

In the three-year curriculum for junior-high-school teachers, electives are not free electives in the usual meaning of that term. The elective studies must be chosen in accordance with specific requirements which are designed to prepare students definitely for teaching the subjects taught in the seventh and eighth grades and in junior-high schools. The electives in this curriculum also provide preparation for teaching the special subjects in the first two years of four-year high schools. The curriculum is also intended to give at least the initial preparation for elementary-school principals.[10]

GENERAL PROVISIONS CONCERNING ELECTIVES

Electives for preparation of junior-high-school teachers are available in this curriculum in the following fields: art, English, French, health and physical education, industrial arts, Latin, mathematics, music, natural science, and social science.[11] All students are required to take a certain amount of work in social science, natural science, mathematics, English, and physical education. They may use the elective privilege to add to these courses a sufficient amount of work so that they will have additional preparation in one or more of three fields. The six semester hours of electives in the first year must be in one of the available electives. In the second year students must elect at least six additional hours in the field chosen in the first year or in one of the other fields. Then three additional hours are added to one of these fields in the third year.

A modification of the three-year curriculum for junior-high-school teachers is made in order to prepare special teachers of art and music.[12] Certain required subjects in the other curriculum are omitted.

Year and Course	No. of Hours
First Year:	
History of Civilization	6
General Science	6
Junior-High-School Mathematics	6
Second Year:	
Modern European History (except students of music)	3
Biology	6
Third Year:	
Diagnostic and Remedial Treatment for Individual Difficulties in English (except students of music)	3
Geography (except students of music)	3
American History and Citizenship (except students of music)	3

[10] *Ibid.*, pp. 8-13.   [11] *Ibid.*, p. 8.   [12] *Ibid.*, pp. 10-13.

In place of the omissions students desiring to specialize in art or music or music and art take the following courses :[13]

Field and Course	No. of Hours
Art	
Public School Drawing	4
Advanced Drawing	4
Nature	4
Mechanical Drawing	6
History and Appreciation of Art	4
Advanced Art Work	4
Advanced Craft Work and Principles of Teaching Art	3
Electives (in art or in the other junior-high-school fields)	15
Music	
Harmony	8
Music Appreciation for the Grades	2
Public School Music	4
Glee Club	2½
Music Appreciation	4
Conducting	1

The general form of the four-year curriculum as finally adopted needs to be presented at this point. The general outline of the four-year curriculum for high-school teachers of history is used for purposes of illustration. All other curricula are similar in their main aspects. This curriculum is as follows:

FOUR-YEAR CURRICULUM FOR TEACHERS OF HISTORY WITH OTHER SUBJECTS IN JUNIOR AND SENIOR HIGH SCHOOLS[14]

FIRST YEAR

	Semester Hours	
	First	Second
Field and Course	Semester	Semester
Education		
Introduction to Teaching	3	
Educational Psychology		3
English		
Current Literature	3	
Composition and Rhetoric		3
Penmanship	(1)o	
Expression		(1)o

[13] *Ibid.*, pp. 10-13.
[14] *Ibid.*, pp. 18-21.

Field and Course	Semester Hours First Semester	Second Semester
Social Science		
History of Civilization	3	3
Natural Science		
General Science	3	3
Mathematics		
Junior High School Mathematics	3	3
Health and Physical Education		
Physical Education	1	1
Orientation		
Personal Hygiene and Social Customs		(1)0
Electives	3	3
	19	19

SECOND YEAR

Field and Course	Semester Hours First Semester	Second Semester
Education		
Secondary Education, Organization and Administration (with special reference to New Hampshire secondary schools)	3	
Educational Sociology		3
English		
Essay and Short Story	3	
Public Speaking and Debate		3
Social Science		
Modern European History	3	3
General Sociology	3	
Natural Science		
Biology	3	3
Health and Physical Education		
Physical Education	1	1
Electives	3	3
	19	19

THIRD YEAR

Field and Course	Semester Hours First Semester	Second Semester
Education		
Principles of Teaching in Secondary Schools..........	3	
History and Organization of New Hampshire Education...		1
Current Educational Problems.....................		1
School Law...		1
English		
Diagnosis and Remedial Treatment for Individual Difficulties in English...........................	3	
Social Science		
Economics..	3	3
Commercial Geography.............................	3	
Commercial History................................		3
American History (Early Period to 1877)............		3
Health and Physical Education		
Physical Education.................................	1	1
Electives...	6	6
	19	19

FOURTH YEAR

Field and Course	Semester Hours First Semester	Second Semester
Education		
Educational Measurements.........................	3	
Conferences..		(3)2
Student Teaching..................................		16
Social Science		
American Government—State and National..........	3	
American History (Later Period from 1877)..........	3	
Philosophy		
Great Philosophers.................................	3	
Health and Physical Education		
Physical Education.................................	1	
Electives...	6	
	19	18

REQUIREMENTS GOVERNING ELECTIVES

In this four-year curriculum for high-school teachers, students are required to select their electives from the following fields: art, English, French, health and physical education, industrial arts, Latin, mathematics, science, social science. Students must take the six semester hours in the first year in one field. They must do the same in the second year. During the four years the electives chosen must include at least twelve semester hours in one field and six semester hours in each of two other fields. Thus students will be prepared to teach history as a first teaching field, some other subject as a second field, and several additional subjects as minor teaching fields.

The four-year curriculum for teachers of English is organized on the same general plan. It is designed to prepare teachers of English and other subjects in junior and senior high schools. Other four-year curricula are organized in commerce, household arts, and mechanic arts. These four-year curricula represent the present point of development of four-year curricula for the preparation of high-school teachers.

PART IV

BASIC POLICIES AND PRACTICES IN TEACHER EDUCATION IN NEW HAMPSHIRE

CHAPTER VIII

THE STRUGGLE FOR UNITY IN THE PUBLIC-SCHOOL SYSTEM THROUGH THE ESTABLISHMENT OF TEACHERS COLLEGES

Previous chapters have detailed the form in which four-year curricula were established in New Hampshire state normal schools. It appears that the state normal schools early had succeeded in providing a sufficient number of teachers for urban elementary schools. At the same time they had supplied a limited number of teachers for rural schools. The first advance after meeting the problem of supplying a sufficient number of urban elementary-school teachers was to move into the junior-high-school field, and for this purpose three-year curricula were established in the two state normal schools. This program was begun before 1919 and was on the way to completion before the advent of the state board of education in 1919. At that time definite preparation was not provided for senior-high-school teachers in a curriculum specifically set apart for that purpose. Commissioner Butterfield from the beginning had been a consistent advocate of state normal schools and their development. Under the stimulus of his interest and with his support and encouragement, the normal schools went forward during the years of his administration as state superintendent of public instruction. In that period they moved toward the objectives of the preceding administration.

Soon after the state board of education was appointed under the new education law of 1919, Commissioner Butterfield began to urge the great importance of teacher education. He formulated a definite philosophy of teacher education as a basis for his recommendations and as a guide for his procedures. He presented to the state board of education a series of reports concerning the preparation of teachers which expressed his philosophy and which were epoch-making in the history of teacher education in New Hampshire. These reports were never published, but they are preserved among the records of the state board of education. They served as a basis for discussion in the meetings of the state board of education and were of incalculable value in creating in the minds of the board an attitude favorable toward needed improvements in the preparation of teachers in the state normal schools and a willingness to approve the necessary expense.

The first of these reports was made in 1920. In it Butterfield made a factual analysis of the needs of the state for teachers and explained the facilities which existed at the two normal schools. This report continued the recommendation to establish three additional normal schools. All these early reports stressed the need for professionally prepared teachers for secondary schools as well as elementary schools.

BASIC PRINCIPLES IN TEACHER EDUCATION

In January, 1922, Commissioner Butterfield placed before the board two postulates as the basis for extending and developing the program of teacher education in the state.[1] The first of these postulates expressed the principle that:

All training of teachers for New Hampshire public schools supported by public taxation must be organized, directed and supervised by the state board of education.[2]

The second postulate proposed that:

The ultimate aim of the state should be that all training of teachers for the public schools at public expense shall be in state training schools, normal schools or teachers colleges.[3]

In support of the first postulate, Commissioner Butterfield called attention to the fact that it represented the expressed will of the legislature. That body had abolished the board of normal-school trustees and had given control of normal schools to the state board of education. It had also discontinued the board for vocational education and had given control of federal aid for the preparation of teachers to the state board of education. It had decreed that all expenditure of public money for preparing teachers for the public-school system should be under the direction of the state board of education. Commissioner Butterfield held that no other position was tenable, for any double system of teacher education would mean duplication of expense. He was emphatic in his statement that a

[1] Butterfield, E. W. *The Training of Teachers for the New Hampshire Public Schools.* Unpublished report presented to the State Board of Education, January 13, 1922.
[2] *Ibid.*, p. 1.　　　　　　　　　　　[3] *Ibid.*, p. 2.

dual system of teacher education would mean the development of two inharmonious and frequently contradictory systems of education in the state. He pointed out difficulties which had already arisen in attempts to develop a unified educational system and explained what conflicts would arise if teachers were trained in two different systems and under two different educational policies.[4] These conclusions seemed to Commissioner Butterfield to represent foundation principles of teacher education which must be observed if the best results were to be attained.

In support of the second postulate, Commissioner Butterfield argued that the training of teachers cannot be successful in an academic college when the department of education in which they receive their professional preparation is merely an adjunct to such an institution. He voiced his conclusions along these lines in the following language:

> The reason is, the teaching spirit which pervades the normal school is absent at the college and knowledge is sought for its own sake. Personal acquisition and not social giving is the keynote. The college student studies history with the constant thought, how does it enrich my knowledge? The normal-school student studies history with the constant thought, how can I present this knowledge to my pupils? Therefore, the college trained teacher teaches subjects rather than children.[5]

NEED FOR TEACHER-EDUCATION POLICY

Commissioner Butterfield called attention to the fact that already other states had transformed their normal schools into teachers colleges, or were considering doing so at an early date. He admitted that at that time New Hampshire did not have facilities for training all its teachers in its normal schools. He nevertheless stressed the need for establishing a policy and indicated what he believed to be the immediate need. He said that first the state

> . . . must make such temporary arrangements as are demanded by economical administration. Its first object, however, is not saving money, but the training of efficient teachers.
>
> It should, therefore, make a careful study of the present situation and of the state needs for teacher training, and should declare its immediate and ultimate policy.[6]

CAMPAIGN OF INFORMATION

In accordance with this principle, Commissioner Butterfield, in succeeding reports, discussed at length the need for professionally

[4] *Ibid.*, p. 2.   [5] *Ibid.*, p. 4.   [6] *Ibid.*, p. 5.

prepared teachers as indicated by factual analysis of the problem, made factual studies of comparative costs of preparing teachers at colleges and at normal schools, pointed out the relative advantages of types of preparation offered at these institutions, and discussed other similar problems. He also kept the board fully informed concerning developments in teacher education in other states throughout the country. These reports served to maintain a lively interest in teacher education among the members of the state board of education and a growing understanding of the problem. In public lectures throughout the state Commissioner Butterfield explained normal schools and the professional preparation of teachers. In this manner he developed throughout the entire state a wholesome concern for better teaching in the public schools, a deep interest in the state normal schools, and a good understanding of their purpose and work. He gave lectures in a large number of communities in which he showed, with lantern slides, pictures of normal-school graduates using progressive methods of teaching in the public schools of the state. Public sentiment in favor of good teaching and a friendly attitude toward the further development of normal schools were thus created. Butterfield was convinced that only an institution designed especially for the preparation of teachers, one which devoted its energies exclusively to that purpose, and in which the curriculum represented professional objectives from beginning to end, could adequately prepare either elementary-school or secondary-school teachers. He talked eloquently and convincingly to the people of the state and to the state board of education concerning the great need to develop at the state normal schools adequate facilities for preparing all the teachers for all the schools of the state.

In a report presented to the state board of education in November, 1922, Butterfield declared that further progress in improving New Hampshire's schools would depend upon better pay for teachers in service, better selection of prospective teachers, and better preparation for teachers.[7] He based his conclusions in part upon a factual study in which he had made an illuminating comparison of salaries of normal-school teachers and those of college teachers, and advocated, for normal-school and college faculties, equality in education, in professional preparation, and in salary. He urged increased appropriations in order to obtain permanent faculties for better teacher

[7] Butterfield, E. W. *New Hampshire's Greatest Need Is Teachers.* Unpublished report to the state board of education. November, 1922.

preparation. He outlined in detail the enlarged facilities which would be needed in each of the two normal schools in order to enable them to prepare an adequate number of teachers for the state. It was in this report that Commissioner Butterfield changed his recommendation concerning the establishment of additional normal schools. Good roads had developed, and travel from one part of the state to another had become easier. These changes seemed to point to the need of developing the facilities of the two existing state normal schools before establishing additional schools. Commissioner Butterfield concluded that:

. . . the state college [later named the University of New Hampshire] should be further developed as a state industrial and academic college and the two normal schools still further developed for the training of teachers.[8]

This report was an outstanding treatise on teacher education and in it foundational principles of teacher preparation in harmony with his philosophy and what facts he was able to secure were enunciated.

INADEQUACY OF A DEPARTMENT OF EDUCATION IN ACADEMIC SURROUNDINGS

On the question of whether or not the state college should be developed into a teacher-education institution, Butterfield took emphatic ground in the negative, saying:

Teachers can not be trained in a department which is an adjunct to an academic college. . . . All experience shows that teachers must be trained in a teaching atmosphere: that a department of education in academic surroundings fails of its purpose.[9]

In his report of November, 1922, Commissioner Butterfield made a strong plea for the preservation of the unity of the public-school system through unity in the preparation of teachers for the public schools. He expressed the matter thus:

The public schools of our state must be a unit. This is possible only when the state board of education supervises not only the elementary and secondary schools of the state but has direction and control over the preparation of all teachers for its schools. Therefore, all training of teachers for New Hampshire public schools supported by public taxation, must be organized, directed and supervised by the state board of education.[10]

Concerning the functions of the state college and the normal schools, Commissioner Butterfield made this pronouncement:

[8] *Ibid.,* p. 9.   [9] *Ibid.,* p. 9.   [10] *Ibid.,* p. 10.

From the first, the normal schools were established to train teachers and for this alone. The college was established to give instruction in agriculture and in mechanic arts. At no time has this natural division been lost sight of by the legislature and no appropriation has ever been given to the college for teacher training. From its general fund the college has properly given courses in education to students who have elected to teach, and to others interested in education, and still continues to do so. The establishment, however, of a department of education at the state college through legislative appropriation, would be a reversal of the state policy for fifty years and would result in a divided control.[11]

It was on December 28, 1925, that Commissioner Butterfield made a positive recommendation that four-year curricula be established at each state normal school with limited enrollments of a few selected students already enrolled in the three-year curricula. He outlined his recommendations in ten definite conclusions, which summarized the situation with reference to teacher education and the need for professionally prepared teachers in the state.[12] Along with these recommendations, Commissioner Butterfield presented another elaborate factual analysis of state needs for teacher preparation, the costs involved, the adequacy of normal-school facilities, and the success already attained in furnishing the state with graduates of two-year and three-year curricula.[13] The adoption of this report consummated the establishment of teachers colleges in New Hampshire. It brought to a close a long struggle to develop teacher-education facilities adequate to furnish the entire state with professionally prepared teachers for every vacancy in elementary and secondary schools.

In December, 1927, as a preliminary to a further discussion of teacher education, the commissioner of education reviewed the state's accomplishments in the preparation of teachers.[14] He reported that at that time the state had succeeded in providing enough two-year graduates for all rural and urban elementary schools and was then also furnishing a sufficient number of three-year graduates for all junior-high-school positions. After stating these facts and show-

[11] *Ibid.*, p. 10.
[12] Butterfield, E. W. *Recommendations to the State Board of Education on Four-Year Courses at the Normal Schools.* Unpublished report to the state board of education, December 28, 1925.
[13] Butterfield, E. W. *The Need of Four-Year Curriculum at the Normal Schools.* Unpublished report presented to the state board of education, December 28, 1925.
[14] Butterfield, E. W. *The School Is Just as Good as the Teacher.* Unpublished report presented to the state board of education, December 6, 1927. Concord, New Hampshire: State Board of Education.

ing that for ten years the state had had enough professionally prepared elementary-school teachers to meet the needs, the report con-
·tinued by saying:

> While this program was being met, we were working upon the problem of
> the rural schools. We quadrupled the accommodations at the normal schools
> and urged country girls to make teaching their life work. We developed
> rural courses and rural training schools at both normal schools. By state
> aid we have helped with salaries and school boards have found in most
> districts desirable boarding homes. For two years we have had trained
> teachers ready for all elementary rural schools.
>
> We have, therefore, fully met our need in three of the four fields. And in
> these fields we now have a surplus of teachers so that careful selection is
> possible.[15]

After summarizing these advances in teacher education, the same
report continues and records the fact that there was a constant short-
age of high-school teachers. Analysis showed that 120 high-school
vacancies were recorded in the latest biennial report, 37 of which
were filled by graduates of New Hampshire normal schools, 19 by
graduates of the University of New Hampshire, 7 by graduates of
other normal schools, and 57 by graduates of other institutions.
That year the state took 64 young graduates of colleges and normal
schools from other states to teach in its high schools.[16] Only a negligible number of these were residents of New Hampshire.

At a meeting in December, 1926, the state board of education
had established four-year curricula in commerce and in mechanic
arts at the state normal schools. It later had added home economics
and other subjects of the high-school program. At the time of the
December report in 1927, a group of students who had already had
two or more years at a New Hampshire normal school were in the
senior year of the new four-year curricula and were expected to
graduate the following June.

DEGREE-GRANTING PRIVILEGE AN INHERENT RIGHT OF THE STATE BOARD OF EDUCATION

The presentation of this report was the occasion for discussing
the question of degrees for the students who were about to graduate
from four-year programs. The state board of education had been
granted in the new education law of 1919 extensive general powers
of control and management of the state normal schools with few

[15] *Ibid.*, p. 1.
[16] *Ibid.*, p. 2.

detailed specifications. These powers were assumed to carry the right to establish four-year curricula. No further legislation was required for that purpose. The question of the right to grant a professional bachelor's degree in education was considered at that time. It was decided that the right to maintain professional schools of college level with four-year post-secondary curricula carried with it the right to confer an appropriate degree in education as an inherent right of the state board of education.

TEACHING SUCCESS OF NORMAL-SCHOOL AND COLLEGE GRADUATES

The report of December 6, 1927, furnished the occasion for discussing the relative efficiency of teachers trained for high-school work in colleges and universities and those prepared in state normal schools. During a large part of Morrison's administration and throughout that of Butterfield, superintendents had been required to furnish ratings of their teachers. The following comparison was made:

The graduates of liberal arts colleges in our public schools are now teaching side by side with the graduates of the normal schools and it is possible to compare the two groups. On pages 114 and 115 of the last biennial report are tables of relative efficiency. These tables are prepared annually from the reports submitted by the superintendents under whom the teachers work and they include all who are teaching their first or second year. The graduates of the liberal arts colleges have had four years of post-secondary education with the maturity which the additional one or two years bring. In spite of this, these graduates every year in teaching worth, lag far behind the teachers trained in normal schools.[17]

A table of average teaching worth, as it was called, based upon superintendents' ratings, was presented in this report, giving the results of the ratings of teachers for eleven years and including the five institutions in which 85 per cent of New Hampshire high-school teachers had received their preparation. This table gave the two New Hampshire state normal schools first and second places with ratings of 81 and 66 respectively. Three colleges occupied third, fourth, and fifth places with ratings of 53, 38, and 26 respectively. Figures were prepared for the year 1926-1927 in which the five institutions maintained the same relative positions with ratings of 79, 73, 46, 29, and 21 respectively. It appears that in the eleven years one New Hampshire normal school had held high place in the an-

[17] *Ibid.*, p. 5.

nual ratings nine times; another New Hampshire normal school six times; one college five times; another college twice; the third college had occupied a high place in no year of the eleven. This comment followed the presentation of the tables:

> The college and university graduates who come to our schools are a selected group. In general, they are alert, attractive young people from homes of sufficient culture to encourage college attendance, and they themselves have shown ability and determination by their completion of a prolonged course of study. In spite of this they fail, not so much from lack of knowledge but from lack of aptitude. They do not know how to teach and they are unwilling to learn. The reason is that most college professors do not believe that teaching is a science as well as an art and so discourage teacher training.[18]

The quotation undoubtedly referred to graduates of liberal-arts colleges who in order to satisfy certification requirements had taken the minimum number of book courses in education. Such people obviously were not professionally prepared teachers in the sense that graduates of a four-year teacher-education curriculum were prepared for their work. Most of these college graduates came from institutions which did not have a school of education.

Many people, perhaps, will question the assumption underlying Commissioner Butterfield's conclusion concerning the comparative merits of teachers prepared in liberal-arts colleges and those educated for teaching in state normal schools. No rating scale or method of measurement has yet been devised by which teaching merit can be absolutely and conclusively determined. The judgments of superintendents who were asked to estimate the comparative teaching worth of normal-school and college graduates were subjective. Superintendents may have been unduly impressed by the ability of normal-school graduates to perform ably under the particular theory and practice of education which prevailed in New Hampshire. Graduates of liberal-arts colleges, of whom the greater number came from outside the state, undoubtedly taught in many cases according to principles of teaching which were quite different from those then current in New Hampshire. It is quite possible that the graduates of liberal-arts colleges, by the fact of their broader preparation along cultural lines, even though they had been subjected to less training in the immediately usable techniques of teaching, may have had potential resources which contributed to a longer period of growth than was true in the case of the normal-school graduates, and which may

[18] *Ibid.*, p. 6.

have made them eventually better teachers. In view of all these facts, some reason exists for doubting the soundness of the conclusion which Commissioner Butterfield reached concerning the comparative teaching worth of normal-school and liberal-arts college graduates.

SMALL COST OF ADDING PREPARATION OF HIGH-SCHOOL TEACHERS IN STATE NORMAL SCHOOLS

This report of December 6, 1927, shows that the reasons which led the state board of education to choose the state normal schools for the preparation of high-school teachers were financial, educational, and administrative.[19]

The report claimed on evidence which seemed to be sound that secondary-school teachers may be trained at a lower cost at state normal schools. The normal schools, it appeared, already had the courses, the faculties, and the practice schools. The report also declared that the moderate additions to equipment and other facilities required for the preparation of senior-high-school teachers would be small as compared with the expense involved in creating these facilities where none already existed. It seemed unnecessary, the report continued, to make any considerable enlargement in the state normal schools. At the time that the four-year curricula were established the needs of the state were being met with reference to rural school, urban elementary-school, and junior-high-school teachers with some surplus. Enough students already enrolled could transfer to the new four-year curriculum for high-school teachers to furnish as many graduates as the normal schools could immediately place. Butterfield summarized the matter as follows:

The additional cost consists of one year of added instruction for some forty students, if this is the number which our ultimate needs show should be annually graduated. A maintenance cost of $140 per student will mean that the fourth year will add a maintenance cost of $6500. For this year and the next, the State Board of Education's budget, as presented to the legislature, proposed an annual increase to the normal school appropriation of $5000.[20]

This New Hampshire experience contributed some evidence which, for one state at least, seemed to indicate that it is possible without great additional cost to make a start in establishing the preparation of high-school teachers in the state normal schools which

[19] *Ibid.,* p. 6.　　　　　　　　　　[20] *Ibid.,* p. 11.

already have three-year curricula and the necessary training schools, libraries, laboratories, buildings, and faculties.

In this connection, it must be said, however, that this view of the comparative cost of preparing secondary-school teachers in normal schools and in liberal-arts colleges probably fails to recognize other factors which deserve consideration. On the one hand, it well could be argued that separate teachers colleges with curricula organized primarily and exclusively for teacher preparation, if the institutions have all the necessary equipment for the adequate education of teachers, might cost more than would liberal-arts colleges for preparation of corresponding length. The greater cost for providing distinctly professional preparation for teachers in teachers colleges could be justified by the social values coming from having well-prepared teachers. If broad cultural education for teachers, which seems to be one predominant desideratum at the present time in the minds of students of the problem, is to be required, it can hardly cost less in one institution than in another, provided that it is equally well done and equally excellent provision is made for it in each institution. Well-prepared faculties, proper libraries, adequate laboratories, suitable buildings, and other forms of equipment can hardly cost less on one campus than on another. For all these reasons, Commissioner Butterfield's contention concerning costs in teacher education cannot be interpreted as conclusive in settling the question on the side of permanently smaller costs for teacher preparation in teachers colleges. He did, however, seem to maintain his point against the alleged large cost of establishing four years of preparation for high-school teachers in normal schools which already were offering three years of such preparation on the basis of fairly adequate equipment for that purpose.

PRESERVATION OF UNITY IN THE PUBLIC-SCHOOL SYSTEM

The second reason given for training secondary-school teachers in state normal schools was the one to which Butterfield had previously referred in passing, namely, preservation of the unity of the public-school system from the first grade to high-school graduation.

MODERN TEACHERS COLLEGE REPRESENTATIVE OF NON-SELECTIVE MASS EDUCATION

This argument was closely related to Bagley's statement made two years later in which he clearly pointed out that in the early history of secondary education in this country both the secondary school and the liberal-arts college were institutions of selective class education. At that time the liberal-arts college could more properly prepare high-school teachers. Later, however, when the high school became an institution of non-selective mass education, the liberal-arts college was poorly adapted to the preparation of secondary-school teachers. The traditions of the liberal-arts college which corresponded fairly well to those of the early secondary schools, were not those of the modern high school when it became an institution for all types of children. The modern teachers college more nearly represented the ideals of non-selective mass education. It became, therefore, a more suitable institution for the preparation of secondary-school teachers.[21]

Butterfield made a plea for teacher preparation exclusively under state control, entirely at state expense, completely managed and administered by the same board which controls and directs all other aspects of public elementary and secondary education in the state. Thus he put into language a principle of teacher education which may be called the principle of unity in teacher preparation.

NECESSITY OF A UNIFIED TEACHER-EDUCATION CURRICULUM

As the third reason for preparing high-school teachers in state normal schools, Butterfield discussed with the state board of education one philosophy of teacher education which holds it to be impossible to prepare teachers most appropriately by first giving them a broad and liberal education and then requiring them to take a few courses dealing with educational psychology and theory and principles of teaching. He pointed out that a considerable number of students of the problem of preparing teachers hold that an adequate teacher-education curriculum must enroll its students at the beginning and carry them through four years in courses especially organized for teacher education and adapted in content and method to that objective. He argued on the basis of his philosophy that high-school subjects must be studied from the point of view of the teacher. A university or college which desires to prepare teachers adequately must have a separate faculty, for academic study in

[21] Bagley, William C. *Significant Trends in Teacher Training.* Unpublished address delivered at the seventy-fifth anniversary of the founding of the State Normal School at Salem, Massachusetts, September 19, 1929.

a liberal-arts curriculum must be superseded by a type of study of subject matter which recognizes the needs of teachers and which will be different both in viewpoint and in organization. An adequate .teacher-education institution must develop practice schools under its own direct control. Butterfield insisted that, without these essentials, teacher education would be ineffective.

POLICIES AND PROCEDURES BASED UPON STUDY OF STATE NEEDS

Commissioner Butterfield proceeded at all times in terms of state needs as revealed by the most penetrating factual studies which he was able to make. It was never his idea that the state normal schools of New Hampshire should admit to preparation for high-school teaching all students who came, and thus function as liberal-arts colleges. He studied the situation in the state and regulated enrollments in terms of what he found. In this connection he said:

> Our problem is based upon dependable data. Each year we need about 400 new teachers for our public schools. This does not include experienced teachers who come to us from other states. The reports for several years show that nearly a fixed number is needed for the several grades and divisions of the elementary schools, and for the different departments of the senior and junior high schools. An enrollment of 1000 permits us to graduate 350 and this is about the number required for our vacancies. The limits of enrollment at the schools [normal schools] may be regarded as between 1000 and 1200 students.[22]

FUNDAMENTAL PRINCIPLES OF ORGANIZATION OF A STATE PROGRAM OF TEACHER EDUCATION

The several reports from which quotations have been presented in the foregoing pages were memorable in the history of teacher education in New Hampshire. They laid down principles which were fundamental in organizing the state program of teacher education. They reviewed for the state board of education the fundamental issues at stake in New Hampshire. Their presentation and the discussion and the final decision to present the degree of Bachelor of Education to the small group of students who were to graduate from four-year curricula in the New Hampshire state normal schools in June, 1928, marked the final stage in the transformation of the state normal schools to the status of teachers colleges, toward which developments had been tending for a number of years.

[22] *Ibid.,* p. 12.

In an address before the New Hampshire state teachers association at its annual meeting in 1927, Commissioner Butterfield discussed the preparation of high-school teachers in the state normal schools.[23] He summarized and elaborated many of the things which he said in his December, 1926, report to the state board of education, and reviewed again the three reasons why the state board of education established the preparation of high-school teachers in the state normal schools. Among other things he said:

> The present decade records the decision of progressive schools that high school teachers, as well as elementary, must be trained for their work. It is agreed that the untrained liberal arts graduate is no more prepared for teaching than for law, medicine, or nursing. As a result, in about forty of the states, high school teachers are now trained in the normal schools in a four-year curriculum.[24]

OPPOSITION BY THE STATE UNIVERSITY TO NORMAL-SCHOOL PREPARATION OF HIGH-SCHOOL TEACHERS

With the establishment of four-year curricula and the decision to grant the degree of Bachelor of Education, the final chapter in the history of the establishment of teachers colleges in New Hampshire was not written. When the plans of the state for an enlarged normal-school program, which included the preparation of secondary-school teachers and the granting of a professional bachelor's degree to graduates of the state normal schools, were announced, the state university registered objections to this policy. The battle was of short duration but vigorously prosecuted. It centered around two events. The first was a conference of high-school principals which was called at the state university. This conference was devoted to the administration, organization, and teaching technique of the high school.[25] It seemed to the commissioner that such a conference conducted by the university faculty with no reference to the state board of education was contrary to the policy of unity in the public-school system.

At a conference between the state board of education, the commissioner of education, and the president of the state university, the president made it very plain that the university believed that the

---

[23] Butterfield, E. W. *The Three Reasons.* Unpublished address delivered at the New Hampshire State Teachers Association, October 30, 1927.

[24] *Ibid.*, p. 2.

[25] Butterfield, E. W. *Unpublished Letter to the State Board of Education.* Dated September 24, 1927. p. 1.

state board of education had the power of management, supervision, and control of the elementary schools, but that the university was particularly responsible for high-school teachers and high-school teaching.[26] The commissioner referred again to his fundamental principle of unity in the public-school system and pointed out that the public schools of the state were organized into elementary schools including the first six grades with class teachers, and secondary schools beginning with the seventh grade and ending with the twelfth, with subject teachers. He again called the attention of the state board of education to the fact that the policy advocated by the university contemplated the division of the public schools into two distinct units with elementary schools directed by the state board of education and secondary schools by the trustees of the state university. Butterfield concluded by saying:

Such a division was not contemplated in our laws and would be a detriment to educational work in the state.[27]

The objection of the university centered in part around the contention that the cost of such normal-school enlargement as was contemplated would be prohibitive.

GREATER COST OF PREPARING HIGH-SCHOOL TEACHERS
AT STATE UNIVERSITY

The proposal of the university to prepare teachers for the secondary schools of the state contemplated using the existing university courses with the additional arrangements for practice teaching in the secondary schools of the state with inspection and supervision by university professors. To this, the commissioner objected on the ground that preparation of secondary-school teachers in subject matter by means of liberal-arts courses, and study of education and practice teaching in the secondary schools of the state did not constitute adequate preparation. The commissioner presented the argument that the university would need to incur considerable additional cost in creating some of the facilities which he regarded as essential in preparing teachers.

The commissioner's report to the state board of education, made on December 28, 1925, and the subsequent action of the board led finally in 1929, after some degrees had been granted to normal-school graduates, to a survey of the state normal schools. After consulta-

[26] Ibid., p. 1.   [27] Ibid., p. 1.

tion among themselves, conversations with some schoolmen in the state, and a conference with the commissioner and the state board of education, the surveyors wrote their opinions concerning what they thought the state ought to do in the preparation of teachers for its public schools.[28]   As their main suggestion, they recommended that all secondary-school teachers be prepared at the state university. This survey constituted the second event in the contest connected with the establishment of teachers colleges in New Hampshire.

SUMMARY OF THE CAMPAIGN TO ESTABLISH TEACHERS COLLEGES IN NEW HAMPSHIRE

The campaign for the establishment of teachers colleges in New Hampshire was based on two fundamental principles of teacher education which Commissioner Butterfield sought to establish in the state.   The first was the principle of unified control of teacher education, which emphasized education as a function of the state and demanded that all teacher education operate under a single educational authority, namely, that which is in control of public elementary and secondary education in the state.   The second principle, merely a corollary of the first, asserted that the necessary and desirable degree of unity in the public-school system can be attained only by placing all teacher education in New Hampshire under the state board of education.   These were the principles upon which Commissioner Butterfield carried on for more than a decade an intensive campaign of education in behalf of his conception of teacher preparation.· His ideals finally prevailed and teacher education went forward in New Hampshire under the principles which he established.

[28] Stearns, Alfred E., Perry, Lewis and Bill, E. Gordon. *Report of the Committee on New Hampshire Educational Survey,* pp. 15-16.   Concord, New Hampshire: State Board of Education. 1929.

CHAPTER IX

SUBJECT MATTER IN THE PREPARATION OF ELEMENTARY- AND SECONDARY-SCHOOL TEACHERS

THE preparation of teachers in subject matter in New Hampshire normal schools is sufficiently unique to deserve special consideration. The curricula which have been presented in preceding chapters show the general arrangement of courses in education and in subject matter, but they indicate nothing of the content of the courses. An inquiry into that aspect of teacher education in New Hampshire seems likely to be productive.

CONCEPTION OF SUBJECT MATTER IN NEW HAMPSHIRE NORMAL SCHOOLS

In the reorganization of the curricula for elementary-school teachers, which took place in the closing years of Morrison's administration, an approach to subject matter was adopted which differed greatly from the earlier procedure in that and many other states. This conception of subject matter in the normal school made a distinct contribution to the theory and the practice of teacher education.

In Chapter V Morrison's reorganization and extension of the program for the preparation of elementary-school teachers was described. There it was noted that a large element in the curriculum was devoted to what was called methodological study of subject matter. What was the nature of this approach? The evidence may be summarized in a brief statement as a point of departure for a more thorough consideration of the problem. Students who were preparing to teach in elementary schools had had in a secondary school four years of general education beyond the level of the schools in which they were to teach. It was assumed, therefore, that their general education was as nearly complete as was necessary or as time would allow. At least it was sufficient to justify an immediate beginning in a kind of study which was devoted exclusively to teacher preparation. The two years of the normal-school curriculum were, therefore, devoted to professional work or to a type of work in subjects not taught in elementary and secondary schools which combined in a single course both professional and academic elements.

An understanding of the conception which gave character to this methodological work may be gained by a study of the descriptions of the courses as they were found in the catalogs of the two normal schools. Several of these descriptions are quoted as the evidence upon which to base a conclusion.

DESCRIPTIONS OF METHODOLOGICAL APPROACH TO SUBJECT MATTER IN THE PREPARATION OF ELEMENTARY-SCHOOL TEACHERS

The catalog of the normal school at Plymouth said this concerning the methodological work in literature:

The foundation of this course is the reading list suggested in the program of studies for the elementary schools of New Hampshire. Besides careful study of all that material, acquaintanceship is required with other works by the same authors, including something of the life of each, and his place in the history of literature. The aim of the course is eventually preparation for teaching. With this object in view, lessons are planned, demonstrated and discussed in connection with the observational and practice work of the training school. The choice of literature for grade work, the art of story-telling, reading aloud, memorizing selections, and dramatization are some of the essentials included.[1]

This is what the Plymouth catalog said concerning the study of arithmetic from the methodological viewpoint:

Arithmetic of the first six grades, as outlined in the State Program of Studies, is presented to the normal school students from the point of view of the teacher. Study of presentation of subject matter, psychology and underlying method, materials of help in teaching the subject, and practice in lesson-planning and presentation make up the work. Little review of subject matter should be necessary, but incidentally, of course, much academic review is involved in pedagogical presentation.[2]

Drawing was one of the courses which was treated from both the academic and the methodological point of view. The manner in which these two kinds of work were combined is brought out in the catalog statement of the content of the course. The description of the work in drawing at Plymouth follows:

The course in drawing aims to give the prospective teacher help and in-

---

[1] "Courses of Instruction—English." *Catalog of the New Hampshire State Normal School at Plymouth*, p. 29. 1919.

[2] "Courses of Instruction—Mathematics." *Ibid.*, p. 37.

spiration in the perfection of her own ability, and to make her efficient in teaching subjects. The course includes free-hand drawing from nature, landscape composition, illustrative sketching and blackboard drawing; color and design to the end of knowing and appreciating problems and principles as applied to school and home decoration and art generally in its various forms. Different forms of handwork and construction adapted to the work of grades are worked out in paper and cardboard and in round table representation. Other work consists of problems in elementary book-binding, weaving and mechanical drawing, the reading and making of working drawings and plans. The entire course is planned to be practical and capable of use in the elementary schools. Student-teachers arrange subject matter, make outlines and lesson plans, and give outlines in all grades.[3]

These are typical descriptions. At Keene a good deal was done in having the normal-school students prepare and present to their classmates for criticism model lessons which represented organization of subject matter suitable for children. This represented undoubtedly an artificial situation. On the other hand, it provided experience in organizing curriculum materials for teaching purposes. Since students, at that same time, had opportunity for abundant contacts with training schools throughout the entire two-year period, this work was in no way regarded as a substitute for actual experience with children. It was supplemental to such work.

SUBJECT MATTER IN THE PREPARATION OF SECONDARY-SCHOOL TEACHERS

In studying the viewpoint which prevailed in the preparation of secondary-school teachers, so far as the approach to subject matter was concerned, it will be in order to present descriptions of a number of the subject-matter courses.

The three basic courses in history are chosen for purposes of illustrating the method of treating subject matter in the preparation of high-school teachers. Descriptions of these courses are quoted:

History of Civilization. The professional treatment of the outline for History of Civilization in the State Program of Studies receives careful consideration. Study is made of advanced historical materials dealing with the units outlined in the State Program.

Modern European History. The professional treatment of the outlines for Modern European History in the State Program of Studies receives careful consideration. Study is made of advanced historical materials dealing with these units.

American History. The professional treatment of the outline for United States Constitutional History in the State Program of Studies receives care-

[3] "Courses of Instruction—Drawing." *Ibid.,* p. 37.

ful consideration. Study is made of advanced historical materials dealing with the units outlined in the State Program.[4]

Three essential facts about the treatment of subject matter appear throughout these descriptions. (*a*) Little or no advanced academic treatment of subject matter is undertaken in any subject prior to the study of the materials of instruction in the high-school subjects which students will teach. (*b*) Nearly all courses in subject matter begin with a consideration of the materials outlined in the state program of studies and in connection with the study of these materials advanced study of appropriate subject matter occurs. (*c*) No special-methods courses are offered.

These are the same principles which have been found in the approach to subject matter in the preparation of teachers for the elementary-school field. This approach seems to represent a universally applied principle in New Hampshire which was established by Morrison and which has persisted to the present day.

STUDY OF SUBJECT MATTER IN THE FIELD OF COMMERCE

The commerce courses may serve as a basis for further discussion of this question. They depart greatly from the usual plan and organization of such courses in teachers colleges. One fact in particular needs special consideration in this connection, for it represents a unique development in teacher education. Only graduates of four-year commerce curricula in secondary schools are admitted to the four-year curriculum for preparation of teachers of commercial subjects in secondary schools. The present writer has examined catalogs of teachers colleges in the United States without finding another state in which this requirement prevails. Students who have taken a four-year commercial curriculum in secondary school as a prerequisite to admission to the four-year teacher-education curriculum in commerce in the normal school have had a great deal of work in commerce which makes possible a very different type of study in the normal school from that which they would take if they had not already had the extended preparation in commerce. Usually they have taken the following courses in high school:

Business forms and related arithmetic (seventh grade)
Elementary bookkeeping (eighth grade)

[4] *New Hampshire Normal Schools. Circular of Information. "Program of Studies: Curricula and Courses,"* p. 54. 1933.

Junior business training with applications of commercial arithmetic
Bookkeeping, first course
Bookkeeping, second course
Commercial geography
Stenography (two years)
Typewriting (two years)
Office practice with application of stenography and typewriting
Business law
Business organization, salesmanship, and advertising
(All these are year-courses when not otherwise indicated.)

Students who have had such extensive secondary-school work in commerce do not need the most elementary courses in the normal school. Since they have already attained certain understandings and acquired certain skills they can start on their professional study at the outset. These students can begin immediately a study of curriculum materials and push back extensively into a background for those materials. That is what is done.

PROFESSIONAL SUBJECT MATTER IN STENOGRAPHY AND TYPEWRITING

Stenography and typewriting are taught in the normal school by their further use in practical situations during the first two years. This is followed by professional treatment of the material in this field as outlined in the state program of studies for high schools, but with further application in actual office work and in correspondence. The following descriptions of the first three years of work in stenography and typewriting bring out this principle:

Office Training. The purpose of this work is to conserve what the student brings from high school in shorthand and typewriting ability, to improve upon it, to give practice in all kinds of office routine and to familiarize with office equipment. All kinds of actual office business are furnished by the several departments of the school.[5]

Application of Stenography and Typewriting. The requirements of this course are: taking of stenographic notes, transcribing, reporting and filing to the end of keeping alive skill in stenography and typewriting.[6]

Stenography and Typewriting and Commercial English. The professional treatment of material in stenography, typewriting and office practice in the State Program receives special emphasis. Further applications are made in office work. Business English and correspondence form an integral part of the work of the course.[7]

[5] *New Hampshire Normal Schools. Circular of Information. "Program of Studies: Curricula and Courses,"* p. 25. 1933.
[6] *Ibid.,* p. 26.
[7] *Ibid.,* p. 27.

SECONDARY-SCHOOL PREREQUISITES IN INDUSTRIAL ARTS

Further discussion of the subject-matter approach in New Hampshire normal schools will utilize the four-year curriculum in trade and industrial (shop and related) subjects for junior and senior high schools. This curriculum has the same unique feature found in connection with the curriculum in commerce. Only graduates of four-year industrial-arts curricula in secondary schools and journeymen (men who have served an apprenticeship of three years in a trade) who have had at least one year of experience in the trade and who can demonstrate ability to do the work are admitted to this curriculum. New Hampshire secondary schools offer four-year industrial-arts curricula. The following subjects are included in this standard curriculum and are taken as a prerequisite to admission to the industrial-arts curriculum in the normal schools:

Manual training and related sketching and drawing (two years—seventh and eight grades)
Home mechanics—general shopwork in wood and metal including electricity
Cabinetmaking
Shop mathematics
Pattern making and moulding
Printing
Automobile mechanics and repairs
Shop electricity
Machine-shop practice (two years)
Shop physics and electricity
Mechanics
Mechanical drawing (four years—two periods a week)
(All these are year-courses when not otherwise indicated.)

Thus the elementary aspects of all the subjects of an industrial-arts curriculum are completed before students enter the normal school. It is unnecessary, therefore, to teach elementary courses in shopwork and drawing. This fact introduces a unique feature into the preparation of special teachers for industrial arts in high schools and shop and drawing and related subjects in vocational schools. It is possible for the normal school, under these conditions, to give a kind of work which differs greatly from the elementary shop and drawing courses usually found in four-year industrial arts curricula in normal schools and teachers colleges. Students in this curriculum can begin professional study at once without waiting to acquire the skills needed in order to be allowed to engage in student teaching.

CONCLUSIONS CONCERNING THE APPROACH TO SUBJECT
MATTER IN NEW HAMPSHIRE NORMAL SCHOOLS

It is now possible to answer the question raised earlier concerning
the nature of the methodological approach to subject matter at the
state normal schools of New Hampshire. The descriptions of the
courses which have been quoted in this chapter and a study of the
catalogs of the New Hampshire normal schools for the ten-year
period following Morrison's reorganization, justify certain conclusions. They are implied in what has already been said, but they
are deemed of sufficient importance to justify reviewing them in
summary form.

1. The initial approach to subject matter in the New Hampshire
normal schools is made through consideration of pupils' materials.
A state program of studies has been in use for thirty or more years
throughout the public elementary and secondary schools in the state.
This program for a long period of years was used as a foundation
for the work of teachers' institutes in which the state superintendent, members of his staff, superintendents, principals, and teachers
discussed and interpreted it as the basic guide for their work. This
same program was used as the curriculum of the training schools in
the state normal schools. It was further used as a basis and point
of departure for subject-matter study in the various normal-school
courses. The study of subject matter in the New Hampshire normal schools begins in practically every case with a study of the
chapter in the state program of studies in that field. That chapter
furnishes the point of departure and also determines to a very large
degree the content which is studied in subject-matter courses. In
other words, the approach to subject matter begins with a consideration of the actual curriculum materials which will later be used in
elementary-school and secondary-school classes. The method of
approach is based upon this question: What understandings and
what background in subject matter are necessary for the teacher's
preparation in order that he may best use these materials?

In beginning with the study of elementary-school or secondary-
school materials the work is not limited to rudimentary subject
matter, but the students delve into the background of materials
needed for the best understanding and the best use of these curriculum materials. In studying advanced materials their useful-
ness in contributing to the education of the pupils is constantly kept

in mind. Thus courses in subject matter in the normal schools provide for concurrent growth in grasp of curriculum materials and advanced background for those materials. This is what was involved in Morrison's methodological approach to elementary-school subjects, in those fields in which subjects were treated from both the academic and the methodological viewpoints. In such subjects as history and Latin three years of work of this kind are required as a minimum. This is expected to give the teacher of a high-school subject the required background and the essential command of curriculum materials needed for teaching in the secondary schools.

The extensive use of the state program as previously indicated gives one great advantage in the fact that every student who goes out from a New Hampshire normal school to teach any particular subject knows very definitely in advance the type of materials which he will need, to use. The state program was made under the direction of the state education department by groups of teachers and is generally used in the schools. In indicates in general the materials which are studied in the various subjects.

This does not mean that absolute rigidity prevails in the curriculum of the public schools of the state. The contrary is the fact. A desirable degree of flexibility is found and individual initiative is encouraged. The program is in no sense stereotyped. As a general guide it does represent desirable materials and educational policies which have been worked out jointly by the teachers of the state over a long period of years. It is a sort of manual of best practice so far as that has been determined by the teachers and administrators of the state. Its use in the normal schools and in the public schools of the state enables young teachers to make quite specific preparation for the work which they will do in the schools in which they will teach. It enables students to plan in advance and organize appropriate materials which they know they will have occasion to use in their own teaching.

Under the plan which has been described a degree of unity has always prevailed in recent years between the normal schools and the public-school system of the state[8] by which a deplorable degree of inco-ordination between normal schools and public schools has been partially resolved. Furthermore, the state normal schools for thirty

[8] Judd, Charles H. "The Isolation of the Normal School—Inco-ordination of Administrative Units." *Problems of Education in the United States,* pp. 44-50. New York: McGraw-Hill Book Company. 1933.

years have been carefully supervised, as has already been mentioned, by the state education department.

2. While the study of subject matter involved a reconsideration of the material of elementary-school subjects, it was not a mere review. It was pedagogical treatment of that material, which meant organizing it into suitable curriculum materials for use in teaching children. Such planning and organization of curriculum materials was a definite feature of all methodological courses.

3. Everything revolved around the training school, which was considered as the integrating force throughout the whole process of the preparation of the teacher. While carrying on methodological study of materials, students were constant participants in the work of the training school. They thus connected their study of subject matter at all times with children's processes and learning. It has already been pointed out that not only did students have regular periods of observation and participation in connection with their courses in education, but they also had a good deal of observation and participation in connection with their other subjects. The critic teachers frequently brought classes of children to the normal-school classrooms and taught them for demonstration purposes before the normal-school students.

4. The participation in teaching individuals and groups of children in the first year and the large amount of responsible student teaching in the second year enabled students to make extensive use of their materials. It was the purpose of the curriculum that students should acquire their understanding of materials and their knowledge of the use of the materials of pupil education by extensive experience in teaching and do it concurrently with teaching.

5. Much less emphasis than is often found was placed on learning subject matter in advance of the need for its use in teaching. Extensive background courses in subject matter apart from the need for its organization for teaching purposes and its use in teaching children were not found. In the direct attack upon children's materials made at the outset such advanced subject matter as was needed was studied at the time and to the extent that it was required. This principle was by no means perfectly exemplified. A distinct tendency in its direction, however, was discernible, beginning in 1916 with Morrison's reorganization.

6. In such subjects as commerce and industrial arts the smaller amount of the technical subjects which is needed is one noteworthy

feature of teacher preparation in New Hampshire. A student who completes the four-year curriculum for teachers of trade and industry or a similar curriculum for high-school teachers of commerce has had eight years of preparation in his special field.

7. The situation which existed in the state normal school at Keene, after Morrison's reorganization, was unique in many particulars at that time and greatly favored this approach to subject matter. Since students at Keene began in their first year to observe in the training school for an hour a week and to spend another hour a week working with pupils individually and in groups, they thus became at the outset actual participants in the group-living going on in the training-school classrooms; they had opportunities at the beginning to come into actual realistic contact with pupils engaged in learning at the very time that in their work in psychology the study of the theory of children's learning was being undertaken; they taught as student-teachers on a full-time responsible basis throughout the second year for two periods of nine weeks each, alternating with periods of study accompanied by observation in the training school. This constant contact with the training school and almost continuous experience in teaching throughout the entire period of preparation kept constantly before students the problem of the need for materials. They lived constantly under the necessity of having a command of curriculum materials available for use in teaching children. They felt at all times the necessity of growing into a command of larger and larger resources in the materials of pupil education. The writer has observed interested groups of these students working for hours after school creating materials for use on the following day in the training-school classrooms. For one group two nine-week periods of study after nine weeks of responsible student teaching made the study significant in a way not possible before any responsible student-teaching was undertaken.

8. About the only difference between the courses which were methodological only and those which were academic and methodological was that the latter carried the view of new material farther than did the former. Students had, at the beginning, somewhat less understanding in the academically treated subjects than in those which were purely methodological.

The conception of subject matter in teacher education which has been discussed in this chapter represents one of the current conceptions in teacher education which has been a controversial subject in recent years and contributes another aspect to the discussion. These ideas may not represent final thought concerning this aspect of teacher preparation. The practice in New Hampshire, however, represents a distinct contrast in comparison with the purely academic treatment of subject matter followed by theoretical courses in methods of teaching which has prevailed to some extent during the past three decades. It may well be that this conception which is so clearly defined in New Hampshire is the precursor of still another and more effective practice.

CHAPTER X

DEVELOPMENT OF ADEQUATE LABORATORY
SCHOOLS

CRITICISM has often been expressed concerning the limited laboratory facilities which normal schools possess, and it has been stated quite emphatically that normal schools must extend their laboratory schools to include city school systems sufficient to make possible more extensive facilities for student teaching. In this connection the developments at Keene in the years directly following 1916 are worthy of careful examination.

The program and policy of teacher education which was established in New Hampshire under the reorganization of 1916 required facilities for student teaching far beyond those found in the greater number of normal schools at that time. The new curriculum which was adopted in 1916 has already been discussed. The large place accorded to student teaching as a factor in the learning processes has been noted.

GENERAL PLAN FOR DEVELOPMENT OF MORE ADEQUATE
LABORATORY SCHOOLS

The establishment of a new state normal school at Keene in 1908 gave the opportunity for a new start on a more nearly adequate basis with reference to laboratory schools. The city school system at Keene, under a five-year contract between the state and the city, was placed completely under the charge of a member of the faculty of the normal school who had the title of director of training. He was also city superintendent of schools, but he was paid wholly by the state and he was in all respects a member of the normal-school staff. Supervisors placed in the several buildings served as critic teachers and supervisors of student teaching. They did a small part of the teaching of the children, an amount considered sufficient in the interest of the children and also adequate for observation by student teachers. The rest of the teaching was done by the student teachers. As a typical situation a six-room elementary-school building with a kindergarten and the first six grades had a kindergarten supervisor and two other supervisors. It was necessary to place in this situation only a half dozen student teachers each of whom did full-time work for eighteen weeks, which was, as previously explained, in addition to the preliminary participation carried on throughout the first year. This was regarded as an ideal training-school situation. The artificiality of many campus training schools was absent. Here were real schools which must be carried on successfully. Both in their preliminary participation in their first year and in their final student teaching, students worked in a natural setting and experienced realities in an actual school system as a going concern.

The training-school organization thus established continued during the first five years of the history of the normal school, and demonstrated beyond a doubt to the members of the state education department the efficacy of utilizing an entire small-city school system as a training school. The critical studies of this situation made by the deputy state superintendent in charge of normal schools contained evidence which seemed to point to the desirability of this kind of training school.[1] The city school system at Keene, the village school system at Plymouth, and the rural schools in adjoining sections of the state and high schools easily accessible to the two normal schools, which were taken over completely by the state and placed entirely under the charge of the normal school, seemed to the state administration to furnish as nearly adequate training-school facilities as the normal schools need or ever will need. All the purposes of training or demonstration schools appear to be served by these city and rural schools. Then too, they seemed to have other great advantages which campus training schools did not furnish. At the present time they are as completely under the charge of the normal schools as are campus training schools. That condition has prevailed from the beginning. The expense of maintaining these schools is considerably reduced. At the establishment of the normal school at Keene, Morrison arranged to have the state enter into a contract with the city by the terms of which the entire city school system should be turned over completely to the state for training-school purposes. Keene had, in 1920, a population of 11,210. Thus the state normal school had ample resources at that time for doing the type of work which the curriculum contemplated. The catalog for 1919-1920 described the laboratory-school facilities thus:

[1] Brown, H. A. *Reports of Inspection of State Normal Schools.* 1913-1917. (Bound typewritten reports in the Office of the State Board of Education.)

The entire elementary system of Keene, comprising 1300 pupils, is under the direction and control of the normal school and is used for practice purposes. This means that we have over forty rooms to which students may be sent for training, and it is never necessary to place two girls in the same room. Practice work with individual pupils is required of every girl for an hour a week in her [first] year, and practice with regular classes for the entire time during half of the senior year.[2]

POSSIBILITY OF NEW TYPE OF TEACHER EDUCATION THROUGH ENLARGED TRAINING SCHOOLS

These laboratory-school facilities were more extensive than those ordinarily found in normal schools at that time. In addition to the forty rooms in the elementary schools the normal school had control of a large junior high school with ten more rooms and an enrollment of about 350 pupils located in its own school building close to the campus of the normal school. Most normal schools have been deficient in facilities for student teaching. In those early days, two decades ago, they often had only a small campus training school in which the number of children was not large, sometimes no greater than the number of students in the normal school. Sufficient and adequate student teaching and other forms of participation could not be developed under these conditions. However, the reverse was true at Keene, and the state was able to establish a new type of teacher education, made possible by these more nearly adequate laboratory school facilities. These improvements in teacher preparation could not have been introduced with the traditional training schools found at most normal schools. Thus, New Hampshire was able, at that time, to go ahead with another feature of teacher education which was not generally found in normal schools throughout the country.

TRAINING SCHOOL ORGANIZATION

The organization of the city school system at Keene at that time as a training school is significant in this connection.[3] It well illustrates the extent and the organization of the laboratory-school facilities which the normal school had in those years. The following plan shows the schools and the number of rooms in each which were used for student teaching:

[2] *Catalog and Circular of Information of the State Normal School at Keene,* pp. 16-17. 1919-1920.
    [3] *Ibid.,* p. 3.

School	Rooms	Grades
South Keene (Rural)	1	I–VI
Four Corners (Rural)	1	I–VII
Pearl	2	I–IV
Washington	4	Kgtn., I–III
Franklin	4	IV–VI
North Washington	2	I–IV
Lincoln	4	I–VI
Tilden	4	I–VI
Fuller	2	I–IV
Symonds	4	I–VIII
Wheelock	12	Kgtn., I–VI
Junior High School	10	VII–VIII
	—	
	50	

ORGANIZATION OF THE SUPERVISORY STAFF

The organization of the supervisory staff of two typical city schools indicates the adequacy of the staff of supervision and throws a good deal of light on the manner in which teacher preparation was conducted. The Wheelock and Washington schools are chosen for purposes of illustration. The Wheelock school had a kindergarten and six grades. A supervisor, who acted also as principal of the building, had charge of the fourth, fifth, and sixth grades. Another had the first three grades. There was also a kindergarten supervisor. The staff also included four teaching assistants, who were graduates of the normal school. They were among the best of recent graduates and served as room teachers. From five to seven student teachers completed the staff of the school.[4] The Washington School, with kindergarten and the first three grades, had a kindergarten supervisor, a supervisor for the first grade, and a supervisor for the second and third grades. The last-named supervisor served as principal of the building.[5] From three to five student teachers completed the teaching staff of the school. Under these conditions, each student had almost 500 hours of actual experience, of which 450 hours were in actual full-time teaching in regular but well-supervised city schools completely under the control of the normal school, with only one student teacher in a room. There was, at this time, an enrollment of 39 students in the second year of the two-year curriculum,[6] which provided over 33 children for every student teacher.

[4] *Ibid.*, pp. 10-11.   [5] *Ibid.*, p. 1.   [6] *Ibid.*, pp. 54-55.

EXTENT OF OPPORTUNITIES FOR STUDENT TEACHING

The standards of the American Association of Teachers Colleges in 1923 required that the number of pupils annually enrolled in the training school should be not fewer than four times the annual number of graduates from the institution.[7] The number of pupils in the training school at Keene at this time was about forty times the annual number of graduates. The present standards of the American Association of Teachers Colleges require at least one full-time training-school teacher in charge of at least thirty children for every eighteen college students, each of whom, during the year, does a total of 90 clock hours of student teaching. The state normal school at Keene had, on this basis, sixty children for every college student doing, during the year, a total of 90 clock hours of student teaching. In other words, Keene had, for every college student doing 90 clock hours of student teaching, more children in the training school than are now required for every eighteen student-teachers. It was thus possible to provide the amount of student-teaching which the curriculum required. At the present time, the Wheelock School, the Central Junior High School, a considerable number of rural schools, and several high schools in the state constitute the laboratory schools of the state normal school at Keene.

GRADUAL INDUCTION INTO TEACHING

Under the conditions which prevailed at Keene, student teachers found themselves at work from the beginning in an actual school system in which they had a responsible part in management and successful conduct. They were zealous for its success. They had a feeling of responsibility. At the same time, however, they had the opportunity to work with experienced and capable teachers, who were near their own age, and who were more nearly at their own level of insight and skill, but from whom they could learn a great deal about teaching. By the method of gradual induction into teaching they were assimilated into this system little by little, and their experiences were considered to be a definite part of the learning process, not only in their courses in education but in their work in subject matter. Student teachers had access to all the members of the faculty as occasion required. Students had regular class work with the general supervisor who had charge of the whole system.

[7] *Yearbook of the American Association of Teachers Colleges*, p. 17. 1924.

[8] *Catalog and Circular of Information of the State Normal School at Keene*, p. 10. 1919-1920.

These periods were devoted wholly to a discussion of the problems which students encountered in their student teaching. That course might well have been called "Problems of Teaching," for that exactly describes its content.

STATE HIGH SCHOOLS AS PARTS OF LABORATORY SCHOOLS

The present status of the training-school facilities in New Hampshire shows a trend in the development of laboratory-school facilities which many students of the subject have advocated in recent years. When the two normal schools began to prepare junior-high-school teachers, and especially when they began to prepare senior-high-school teachers, the necessity for the extension of laboratory-school facilities became apparent. It seemed desirable to send student teachers into schools closely connected with the normal school. For that reason contracts were made with five high schools in the state which were placed completely under the control of the normal schools as laboratory schools. Each of these high schools is in the charge of a supervisor who acts as principal. The supervisors and the student teachers serve as the staff of the high school and do all the teaching. Students are assigned to these high schools for two periods of nine weeks each. They serve all day daily; they live in the community; they have regular classes in education under the supervisor-principal; they join with the supervisor-principal in community activities; they do not leave the community until their period of teaching is finished.[9]

This extension of training-school facilities did not consist merely in securing permission to do practice teaching in public high schools. On the contrary the state completely took over several small high schools and conducted them as laboratory schools. The normal schools have complete control of these high schools. One member of the faculty of the normal schools serves jointly for the two normal schools as a general supervisor of these off-campus high schools in addition to the supervisor-principals in charge of each school. Two of them were new high schools established in the state. The other three were already in operation and were taken over by the state. The evidence indicates that the management of these high schools as laboratory schools for the normal schools meets with the full approval of the several communities. It will be possible for

[9] "Practice Teaching." *Catalog and Circular of Information of the New Hampshire State Normal School at Keene*, pp. 17-18. 1931.

the state, in the same manner, to have control of whatever elementary schools or secondary schools in the state it may need at any time for laboratory-school purposes. All these steps, in taking over and managing rural, village, and city schools, including high schools, as integral parts of laboratory-school facilities of the normal schools in New Hampshire, points to one way in which teachers colleges may secure the laboratory-school facilities which are deemed necessary in modern teacher education.

When the state first began to extend the laboratory-school facilities of the normal schools to include secondary schools in the state, the commissioner described the first venture as follows:

> The town of Orford is the center of a section of the state which has been without high school facilities since the closing of Orford Academy many years ago. A co-operative arrangement has now been made between the school district of Orford and the Plymouth Normal School so that in the old academy building has been established the Orford High School. This high school offers a full program and will serve as a training school for Plymouth seniors who are preparing for high school teachers. The teaching will be by cadets, supervised from the normal school, and directed by an experienced and very competent critic teacher. The State Board is following this experiment with great interest.[10]

Several years later when this plan had passed the experimental stage, it was again mentioned in the report of the commissioner of education, and his description of it confirms what has just been said concerning it. This is the statement:

> In 1925, a high school was established by the state in Orford, a town without high school facilities. This was made possible by a co-operative agreement between the state and the school district. A skilled critic teacher was put in charge, a schoolhouse equipped and a dormitory for critic and student teachers rented. All teaching has been done by student teachers from the four-year normal school classes, but all work is planned with the critic teacher and is guided by her. There has resulted one of the most successful and well taught small high schools in the state. The people of the community have given this school high approval.
>
> A year later a second school similar in situation was started in Dalton, where the Town Hall became the schoolhouse, and the Grange Hall, the dormitory for critic and student teachers. This school is developing steadily.
>
> In 1929, Acworth High School and the Hampstead High School became training schools for high school teachers by the same plan, and to this list the Hancock High School will be added in 1930-1931.
>
> These five high schools will give full opportunity for the training of senior high school teachers under conditions similar to those in other small high

[10] Butterfield, E. W. *Report of the State Board of Education,* p. 139. 1924-1926.

schools of the state. The plan and its results have won expressed appro-
bation by students of education.[11]

USE OF STATE RURAL SCHOOLS AS TRAINING SCHOOLS

The plan for carrying on student teaching in rural schools which
was adopted in New Hampshire is worthy of careful consideration.
In 1931, the catalog of the state normal school at Keene recorded
the fact that thirteen rural schools were completely under the charge
of the normal school as laboratory schools. Student teachers went to
these schools and were the only teachers. In the curriculum for
elementary-school teachers fifty-two students secured that year nine
weeks of full-time, all-day responsible student teaching in one-room
rural schools. These schools were near the normal school and were
supervised co-operatively by the district superintendent of the union
in which they were located and by a special supervisor from the normal school who devoted her entire time to that supervision.[12] The
catalog announced the plan of rural cadet teaching in these words:

Beginning September, 1924, a plan was inaugurated of sending seniors to
rural schools in the vicinity to take entire charge of small rural schools for
a period of nine weeks each. Eleven schools were maintained in this manner
during the year and supervised co-operatively by a special rural critic teacher
and the regular superintendent of schools. The students were most enthusi-
astic and the parents well pleased. At the present time 13 schools are being
conducted on this plan, giving 52 elementary seniors nine weeks each of rural
training—more than eighty seniors asked for these appointments the second
year. This plan has largely solved the difficulty of getting graduates to
teach in rural schools.[13]

The commissioner of education described the rural training schools
and expressed approval of the plan. He said:

Each school has, in towns convenient of access, twelve to fifteen of these
schools and employs a critic teacher whose entire time is given to this group
of schools. It will be seen that these students have taught for nine weeks in
the practice schools of Keene or Plymouth and after this for nine weeks are
given entire charge of a typical rural school. Superintendents report very
favorably on the results obtained by these graduates in their first year of
work.

A considerable number of students from both schools serve as cadet teachers in the elementary and high schools of a number of towns and cities.
Their work is supervised as is the case with the rural cadets.[14]

[11] Butterfield, E. W. *Report of the State Board of Education*, p. 142. 1930.
[12] *Catalog and Circular of Information of the New Hampshire State Normal
School at Keene*, p. 28. 1931.   [13] *Ibid.*
[14] Butterfield, E. W. *Report of the State Board of Education*, p. 139. 1924-1926.

STATE SUPERVISOR AIDS IN TEACHER PREPARATION

The plan for the preparation of teachers for mechanic arts in secondary schools illustrates a principle of teacher education which is worthy of consideration in this connection. The four-year curriculum for mechanic-arts teachers is discussed in another chapter. The manner of conducting student teaching in that curriculum is the subject of interest in this chapter. The state supervisor of high-school work in mechanic arts is a member of the state department of education and works under the direction of the commissioner. Student teaching in mechanic arts is done in the various high schools which offer curricula in that field. The young men who are preparing to be teachers of mechanic arts go into these high schools and teach under the direct supervision of the state supervisor of mechanic arts. This same supervisor has earlier nominated the most promising high-school seniors in those same curricula as applicants for admission to the state normal school which provides that type of preparation. His acquaintance with these students begins, then, not later than their senior year in high school. He has contacts with them throughout their period of preparation in the normal school prior to the time that he becomes their supervisor in their student teaching in their senior year.

It is required that each student who is preparing to be a teacher of mechanic arts shall spend a period in work in industry. This is an actual part of the curriculum for which credit is given. Such students are absent for at least a semester and this counts as one semester of their preparation. The state supervisor of mechanic-arts secures places for these students in industry and supervises their work while they are thus engaged.

This experience in New Hampshire, in organizing more adequate laboratory-school facilities and putting into operation procedures in teacher education which were made possible by these extensions of training schools, established principles which have considerable guidance-value in planning teacher-education programs at the present time. Moreover, these principles and their successful application contribute significantly to the insight and understanding in teacher education in the further development of policies and practices in that field. They do not, of course, afford a complete solution of the laboratory-school problem.

PART V

ACCOMPLISHMENTS IN TEACHER EDUCATION
UNDER A HIGH DEGREE OF CENTRALIZATION

CHAPTER XI

PROGRESS TOWARD REALIZATION OF GOALS OF TEACHER EDUCATION

IT REMAINS now to record progress and achievements, to indicate failures and the causes, to recount difficulties and the solutions which were achieved in the history of teacher education in New Hampshire. It is only incidental to this study to show the relationship of what has happened to centralization in administrative control of teacher education. This chapter presents a summary of the results attained.

For the earliest part of the history of teacher education in New Hampshire, complete and accurate data are not available. Some information, however, was collected in those years and it serves a very valuable purpose in revealing many important facts concerning the situation at that time. Reports were required of school boards from the beginning. These reports fail, however, to include data on the entire teaching staff.

A DECADE OF LITTLE PROGRESS IN TEACHER PREPARATION

Figures for the period prior to 1900 would have little value, for developments and innovations which occurred before that time do not have great significance for this study. Data are presented at this point as a record of what happened during the years from 1900 to 1910 in the improvement of the teaching staff in education and professional preparation. A decade of progress is shown in the following statement which indicates the per cent of teachers in each year who had different stated degrees of preparation:

Extent of Preparation of Elementary-School Teachers	1900	1902	1904	1906	1908	1910
Not graduates of high school or academy.	26.2	25.2	25.8	17.8	15.1	15.1
Graduates of a normal school	13.9	16.7	19.3	18.2	17.7	15.2
Graduates of a city training school	13.3	16.3	18.2	14.6	14.5	10.4
Graduates of a college	7.5	5.2	4.4	2.9	2.9	2.2
Number of different elementary-school teachers	2572	2228	2201	2614	2655	2762*

* "Statistical Tables." *Reports of Superintendent of Public Instruction.* 1900-1910.

During this decade a marked reduction occurred in the per cent of teachers who were not graduates of a high school or academy. At the same time a small gain was made in the per cent of teachers who were graduates of a normal school. This table does not account for all teachers in the state except in the total. The group who were not graduates of high school or academy undoubtedly included teachers with all degrees of education. Many were not even graduates of the elementary school.

It would probably be a fair estimate to say that in 1900, 750 to 1000 high-school graduates with little or no additional preparation were teaching in the state. It is likely that by 1910 the number of high-school graduates with little or no other education had increased to something like 1000 to 1200. In 1900, 700 teachers with professional preparation gained in either normal school or city training school were teaching in the elementary schools. A decade later this number had increased to only 707, which represented a decrease of 1.6 per cent of professionally prepared teachers in the total number of teachers. Although the number of normal-school graduates, as compared with graduates of city training schools, had increased slightly, the decrease in city-training-school graduates largely offset the increase in normal-school graduates. This table thus shows practically a stationary situation with reference to filling the elementary schools with teachers who had professional preparation.

EFFECTS OF NEW NORMAL-SCHOOL POLICY

Beginning with 1912, data were gathered on a different basis to show the number of teachers who were high-school graduates but who had no preparation beyond the secondary school. Information was also secured concerning the number of teachers who had no education beyond the elementary school. These data are presented as the best available record of progress for the period which they cover. These are the facts expressed in per cents:

Extent of Preparation of Elementary-School Teachers	1912	1914	1916	1918
No education beyond the elementary school............	6.8	5.3	4.4	2.6
Secondary-school graduation, but nothing more..........	42.7	36.6	35.6	30.7
Normal school graduation............................	28.0	30.4	39.4	41.6
College graduation..................................	2.8	1.9	1.8	2.3
Post-college education..............................	0.0	0.0	0.0	0.0
Number of different elementary school teachers..........	2539	2682	2493	2473[*]

* "Statistical Tables." *Reports of the Superintendent of Public Instruction.* 1912-1918.

These figures show three significant trends, namely: (*a*) the rapid decrease in the most poorly educated group of teachers who had no education beyond the elementary school; (*b*) a correspondingly rapid decrease in teachers with no education or professional preparation beyond the secondary school; (*c*) a very rapid increase in the number of normal-school graduates, which amounted to a gain of 13.6 per cent in the period of six years.

The year 1912 saw 712 normal-school graduates teaching in the elementary schools. Six years later in 1918 the number of such teachers in these schools had risen to 1,129, a record of substantial progress. It shows the effect of the new normal-school policy which had been inaugurated in the beginning of Morrison's administration and which had resulted in the establishment of the new state normal school at Keene.

In certain years, data were gathered concerning the number of city-training-school graduates. In 1912 the record shows 350 such teachers in the state. This dropped to 256 in 1914 and to 109 in 1916. After that no information is available. It is assumed, however, that the number was negligible after that date, for no further reference was made to that group.

The number of teachers with partial secondary education was recorded for several years during this period. In 1912, 148 such teachers were found in the elementary schools. The number had risen to 383 in 1914 but declined to 360 in 1916. It is natural that this figure should increase as the number with no education beyond the elementary schools decreased. It meant that teachers were going forward with their education and more and more were going through high school and taking two years of normal-school education.

For the years between 1918 and 1922, comparable data are not available. The new state board of education with an enlarged staff came into office in 1919. During the period of reorganization immediately following that time data were not published in a form which admits of ready comparison with previous figures.

EDUCATION OF ELEMENTARY-SCHOOL TEACHERS IN THE PERIOD AFTER REORGANIZATION

Beginning with 1922, after the reorganization had gone fully into effect, more nearly complete statistics were gathered. Figures are available for the next thirteen years which make possible a detailed study of gains in the education of teachers during that time. These figures show some very interesting facts. The figures that follow set forth the extent of the academic education of elementary-school teachers in New Hampshire throughout this thirteen-year period:

Extent of Academic Education of Elementary-School Teachers	1922	1924	1926	1928	1930	1932	1934
One-Room Rural Schools							
Elementary education only	3.1	2.5	2.4	2.3	1.9	1.8	1.9
Partial high school	10.7	10.2	7.9	6.5	4.8	4.4	3.2
High school graduation	80.8	83.9	86.5	88.6	91.9	90.4	88.8
Partial college education	4.6	2.7	2.4	1.5	0.5	1.9	1.3
College graduation	0.8	0.7	0.8	1.1	0.9	1.5	4.6*
Post-collegiate education	.0	.0	.0	.0	.0	.0	0.2
	100.0	100.0	100.0	100.0	100.0	100 0	100.0

* 1.1 per cent of these had 2 or 3 years of normal school work credited toward college degree.

Village Elementary Schools							
Elementary education only	1.1	1.0	1.3	1.1	1.0	0.2	0.1
Partial high school	3.4	3.4	3.6	2.7	2.2	1.5	1.6
High school graduation	89.4	88.6	89.4	90.2	91.3	92.0	89.4
Partial college education	3.8	3.5	3.0	2.7	1.7	1.5	1.8
College graduation	2.3	3.4	2.5	3.3	3.8	4.3	6.5*
Post-collegiate education	.0	0.1	0.2	.0	.0	0.5	0.6
	100.0	100.0	100.0	100.0	100.0	100.0	100.0

* .7 per cent of these had 2 or 3 years of normal school work credited toward college degree.

City Elementary Schools							
Elementary education only	1.0	.0	.0	0.5	0.2	0.2	0.1
Partial high school	1.6	1.1	1.1	0.6	0.4	0.7	0.4
High school graduation	92.4	92.4	91.1	92.2	93.4	91.3	91.2
Partial college education	2.9	2.7	2.5	1.9	1.5	1.7	1.8
College graduation	2.1	3.5	5.2	4.7	4.5	5.6	5.8*
Post-collegiate education	.0	0.3	0.1	0.1	.0	0.5	0.7†
	100.0	100.0	100.0	100.0	100.0	100.0	100.0

* .8 per cent of these had 2 or 3 years of normal school work credited toward college degree.

† Pringle, James H. "Teachers." *Report of the State Board of Education*, p. 51. 1934.

This table refers to education only and does not include professional preparation. It is a record of progress. These figures show in the first place the practical elimination of teachers who had an academic education which included less than secondary-school graduation. Those of that class who remained were certain veteran teachers who had attained by examination or otherwise the highest grade of state certificate. It is worthy of note that in 1934 the per cent of teachers in the one-room rural schools who had attained high-school graduation was only slightly less than the number in village or city elementary schools.

PROFESSIONAL PREPARATION OF ELEMENTARY-SCHOOL TEACHERS AFTER REORGANIZATION

The extent of professional preparation of elementary school teachers after 1922 is recorded in the figures shown in the following tabulation:

Extent of Professional Preparation

of Elementary-School Teachers	1922	1924	1926	1928	1930	1932	1934
One-Room Rural Schools							
None	33.8	16.2	12.7	8.9	5.8	7.1	7.4
Six weeks	31.6	26.1	10.3	6.1	4.2	2.7	2.3
Twelve to thirty weeks	14.9	30.3	35.4	21.4	13.5	12.4	8.8
One year	4.2	7.5	6.8	7.2	3.3	2.9	5.3
Normal school graduates	15.5	19.9	34.8	56.2	73.2	75.0	76.2
Village Elementary Schools							
None	15.8	8.6	5.7	5.2	5.7	6.2	5.1
Six weeks	15.2	8.6	7.2	5.1	3.8	2.3	3.6
Twelve to thirty weeks	13.6	21.6	18.1	15.5	12.6	13.1	10.1
One year	5.8	7.0	4.0	5.0	3.8	4.3	4.3
Normal school graduates	49.6	54.2	64.9	69.2	73.9	75.1	76.9
City Elementary Schools							
None	9.3	8.1	7.5	5.5	4.7	5.1	4.8
Six weeks	3.7	2.9	4.7	3.4	3.4	3.7	3.7
Twelve to thirty weeks	4.7	5.7	5.5	4.7	4.3	4.7	4.0
One year	1.0	4.3	3.5	4.6	4.2	3.5	4.5
Normal school graduates	81.3	78.8	78.8	81.7	83.4	83.0	83.0*

* Pringle, *op. cit.*, p. 52.

This table shows significant results of the teacher-education policy of the state. The most conspicuous fact relates to the number of professionally prepared teachers in one-room rural schools. In 1922 about one-third of the teachers in one-room rural schools had no professional preparation, although more than three-fourths of them were high-school graduates. Almost two-thirds of the teachers in these schools had no more than six weeks of professional preparation. Only about one-seventh were normal-school graduates. Twelve years later the group with no professional preparation had almost disappeared. Instead of two-thirds, only about one-tenth of these teachers had had no more than six weeks of professional preparation. The number of graduates of a normal school with two years of professional preparation had risen from 15.5 per cent to 76.2 per cent. This represents a gain of about 250 per cent in ten years. The per cent of normal-school graduates in city elementary schools in 1922 was more than five times as great as the per cent in one-room rural schools. The per cent in village elementary schools was about three times as great. In 1934, only ten years later, the one-room rural schools had just about as great a per cent of normal-school graduates as the village elementary schools, and only a slightly smaller per cent than city elementary schools.

These facts represent remarkable progress in staffing the rural schools of a state with normal-school graduates. It shows that when a state determines to equalize educational opportunities between one-room rural schools and city elementary schools by furnishing the rural schools with teachers trained equally as well as those provided for city schools, it can do that if it organizes the proper type of work, provides the administrative machinery, and secures the kind of professional leadership necessary for the accomplishment of that end. The staffing of the rural schools of the state with professionally prepared teachers was one of the distinctive achievements accomplished under the new type of centralized administrative control of education which went into effect in 1919 in New Hampshire.

INCREASE IN SCHOOLING OF ELEMENTARY-SCHOOL TEACHERS AFTER REORGANIZATION

It is interesting to study the gains in the total amount of schooling of elementary-school teachers, for, in this consideration, both education and professional preparation are combined. The accompanying table records the increase which occurred in about a decade in the schooling of elementary-school teachers. These figures are available for only nine of the ten years. The state education department in 1926 began for the first time to report figures on this basis. The facts in connection with the nine-year increase in the education of elementary-school teachers in New Hampshire are set forth according to the type of school taught and the per cent of teachers at various levels of educational achievement.

Years of Schooling of Elementary-School Teachers	1926	1928	1930	1932	1934
One-Room Rural Schools					
8 years	3.9	3.9	3.3	2.1	2.3
10 years	5.3	4.4	3.3	2.7	1.7
12 years	53.9	34.2	19.1	14.3	15.2
14 years	35.8	56.2	73.4	79.0	74.7
16 years	1.1	1.3	1.0	1.9	6.1
Village Elementary Schools					
8 years	1.4	1.3	1.4	0.3	1.3
10 years	1.8	2.2	1.8	0.9	1.1
12 years	27.0	23.3	18.0	18.0	14.3
14 years	67.1	69.6	75.0	73.0	73.8
16 years	2.6	4.0	3.8	7.8	10.5
City Elementary Schools					
8 years	0.1	0.4	0.4	0.3	0.1
10 years	0.1	0.1	0.2	0.0	0.1
12 years	15.2	13.0	11.0	9.4	10.3
14 years	77.3	81.0	83.0	81.3	79.7
16 years	7.2	5.5	4.5	9.0	9.8*

* Pringle, James N. *Op. cit.*, p. 48; and chapters entitled "Teachers" in other Reports of the State Board of Education for 1926–1934.

The figures which have just been presented show almost as great a length of preparation for teachers of one-room rural schools as for teachers in village elementary schools. The rural schools are only a little behind city elementary schools. The beginnings of a group of teachers with four years of preparation not only in the village and city elementary schools but also in one-room rural schools appear in this table.

It is now possible to offer a summary of gains in years of schooling of all elementary-school teachers for the period 1926-1934. The facts come from the two previous tables. This table shows the per cent of all elementary-school teachers who had in each year the indicated amount of education and professional preparation. These are the facts expressed in per cents:

Extent of Schooling of Elementary-School Teachers	1926	1928	1930	1932	1934
8 years	1.6	1.7	1.5	.7	.7
10 years	2.2	2.0	1.6	1.0	.9
12 years	30.8	22.4	15.6	13.6	12.9
14 years	61.5	70.1	78.0	77.9	76.4
16 years	3.9	3.8	3.3	6.8	9.1
	100.0	100.0	100.0	100.0	100.0*

* *Ibid.*, p. 48; and chapters entitled "Teachers" in other Reports of the State Board of Education for 1926–1934.

The rapid decline in the number of teachers with only twelve years of schooling is apparent. Substantial gains are evident in the groups with fourteen and sixteen years of preparation. In 1926 only 65.3 per cent of all elementary-school teachers had fourteen or more years of schooling, but in 1934, 85.5 per cent had that amount of preparation. This represented a gain of over 20 per cent in nine years.

EDUCATION OF SENIOR-HIGH-SCHOOL TEACHERS AFTER REORGANIZATION

The fact that one-third of the senior-high-school teachers are shown in the following table as high-school graduates indicates that a considerable number must be normal-school graduates. The remainder are largely college graduates or college postgraduates. This table needs to be considered in connection with the next table which shows the professional preparation of senior-high-school teachers. The relative decrease in per cent of teachers with partial or complete college education is evidence of the increase in the number of those who are normal-school graduates.

Extent of Education of Senior-High-School Teachers	1922	1924	1926	1928	1930	1932	1934
Elementary education only	0.0	0.0	0.1	0.4	0.1	0.4	0.4
Partial high school	0.0	0.1	0.6	1.1	1.3	1.5	0.7
High school graduation	16.2	25.6	27.6	28.1	28.8	28.2	28.9
Partial college education	12.4	4.4	3.7	3.6	2.7	2.4	2.3
College graduation	68.6	67.6	65.4	62.1	60.9	60.3	57.1
Post-collegiate education	2.8	2.3	2.6	4.7	6.2	7.2	10.6
	100.0	100.0	100.0	100.0	100.0	100.0	100.0*

* Pringle, *op. cit.*, p. 51.

PROFESSIONAL PREPARATION OF SENIOR-HIGH-SCHOOL TEACHERS AFTER REORGANIZATION

The following figures show the extent of professional preparation of senior-high-school teachers:

Extent of Professional Preparation of Senior-High-School Teachers	1922	1924	1926	1928	1930	1932	1934
None	67.4	48.8	38.0	35.7	36.2	33.4	32.3
Six weeks	10.0	13.4	20.8	19.3	17.4	17.9	16.0
Twelve to thirty weeks	6.1	13.2	16.5	18.6	19.5	21.7	20.2
One year	1.3	4.4	2.8	5.0	2.5	2.4	4.2
Normal-school graduates	15.2	20.2	21.9	21.4	24.4	24.6	27.3
	100.0	100.0	100.0	100.0	100 0	100.0	100.0*

* *Ibid.*, p. 52.

This is a record of thirteen years of progress. In 1922, two-thirds of all senior-high-school teachers had no professional preparation, while thirteen years later only about one-third were entirely lacking in such preparation. In 1922 only one-sixth of all the high-school teachers had from six to thirty weeks of professional preparation, but by 1934 about two-fifths had that amount of preparation. The percentage of normal-school graduates teaching in senior high schools rose from 15.2 to 27.3 in the thirteen-year period. This represented a gain of about 12 per cent. It appears that during this decade the high schools of the state greatly increased their dependence on the normal schools in filling their vacancies.

GAINS IN YEARS OF SCHOOLING OF SECONDARY-SCHOOL TEACHERS

A summary of the gains in years of schooling of secondary-school teachers for the period 1926-1932 is presented:

Extent of Preparation of Secondary-School Teachers	1926	1928	1930	1932	1934
8 years	.1	.6	.6	.5	.2
10 years	.2	.6	.6	.7	.8
12 years	7.9	7.7	5.5	5.6	4.8
14 years	22.9	22.2	26.1	13.9	11.1
16 years	68.9	68.9	67.2	79.3	83.1
	100.0	100.0	100.0	100.0	100.0*

* *Ibid.*, p. 48; and chapters entitled "Teachers" in other Reports of the State Board of Education for 1926–1934.

This table combines the facts of the two preceding tables. It shows a substantial increase in the number of teachers in secondary schools who have had four years of preparation. The gain was over 13 per cent. The fact that a good many graduates of three-year curricula in normal schools went into service in secondary schools tended to hold in those schools a large group of teachers who had not had four years of preparation beyond secondary school. Some two-year normal-school graduates were employed in the high schools of the state, especially in art, music, and household arts. These teachers were professionally prepared and were probably successful in their special field. It is probable that all but about 10 per cent of all senior-high-school teachers were college graduates or graduates of a two-year or a three-year curriculum in a state normal school. In recent years most of the normal-school graduates had had three years of preparation.

During the years from 1922 to the present time the secondary schools of the state were in a transitional period with reference to teacher education. Morrison and Butterfield had assembled extensive factual records concerning the poor teaching of college-prepared high-school teachers who had had little or no professional preparation. Both these men had set themselves to the task of building a system of state normal schools. A decided preference appeared among public-school administrators for teachers with normal-school preparation. The extension of curricula in the normal schools to provide for the preparation of high-school teachers went forward during Butterfield's administration, and high schools began to employ more and more normal-school graduates, beginning with a few who had two years of such preparation, later employing many who had taken a three-year curriculum, and finally selecting only those with four years of such preparation. The present requirements exclude from teaching in senior high schools any teachers who have not had four years of academic and professional preparation.

It is required that all candidates for secondary-school positions, after July 1, 1935, shall have had twelve semester hours of work in education, and after July 1, 1936, they shall be prepared in three fields and may teach only those subjects. Candidates must pass examinations in the secondary-school program of studies and in school law. Examinations are required in methods of teaching, educational psychology, and secondary-school management. Candidates may, however, present college credits for these subjects.

SUMMARY OF GAINS IN EDUCATION AND PROFESSIONAL PREPARATION OF TEACHERS

It will be interesting to note the gains made in education and professional preparation of all teachers in both elementary and secondary schools in New Hampshire. A summary of these gains for the thirteen-year period from 1919 to 1932 is presented:

Extent of Preparation of Teachers	Per Cents 1919	Per Cents 1934	Per Cent of Gain or Loss
Graduates of New Hampshire normal schools	22.7	54.5	177.1 (Gain)
Graduates of other normal schools	9.2	9.3	14.9 (Gain)
Graduates of colleges	18.0	23.1	21.8 (Gain)
Teachers with some college or normal school study but not graduates	15.7	11.3	17.8 (Loss)
Teachers with no post-secondary study or professional preparation	34.4	1.8	54.0 (Loss)*

* Pringle, James N. "Teachers." *Report of the State Board of Education*, p. 48. 1934.

These figures express significant facts. The first is the great gain in the number of graduates of New Hampshire normal schools, which amounted to 177.1 per cent during this period. The gain in the number of teachers who were graduates of normal schools in other states amounted to 14.9 per cent. The gain in the number of college graduates was 21.8 per cent. The number of teachers who had done some college or normal-school study, but who were not graduates, showed a substantial loss. There was a decrease of 54 per cent in the number of teachers with no post-secondary study or professional preparation. The most significant fact shown in this table is the state's great dependence upon normal schools for teachers for both elementary and secondary schools.

These facts are an indication of the great gains in the service which the normal schools rendered to the state. This all came after the establishment of the type of centralized control and administration which was inaugurated with the advent of the state board of education in 1919. It is impossible to say with absolute certainty that these gains would not have come under the former type of administration. A study of the whole situation, including the records of progress which were made both before and after 1919, indicates, however, the clear improbability that they would have happened under the old régime. The fact that the same commissioner of education and in general the same staff of administrative officers were at the head of educational affairs before 1919 as well as after that date is a strong indication that the new type of centralized administrative control may have been in large measure responsible for the gains in teacher education.

CHAPTER XII

A UNIFIED STATE PROGRAM OF EDUCATION AND CERTIFICATION OF TEACHERS

THE preceding chapters have pictured a state system of education which began in almost complete decentralization, which at first advanced to a measure of centralization through educational leadership in the state education department, and which finally emerged into complete statutory centralization of control and administration. The facts which have been presented have indicated a slow but steady growth toward a type of control of teacher education which has certain distinctive features.

Teacher education in New Hampshire began in a teachers-seminary extension of the common school. It had an early disjunctive development with little or no relationship to secondary schools and none with institutions of college rank. After a long period of disjoined development under a policy of decentralization in state educational administration it came to its present unification in teachers-college status under a high degree of centralized state educational control and administration.

A HIGH DEGREE OF CENTRALIZED CONTROL OF TEACHER EDUCATION

The author of this dissertation has searched catalogs of state normal schools and teachers colleges and state education reports exhaustively in an effort to find other state systems of education in which so great a degree of unity prevails so far as teacher education is concerned. The state laws of those states which are known to have a high degree of centralized control have been examined for this same purpose. This fact gives point to the original questions of this dissertation: What has happened in teacher education under these conditions? What results have been secured? What failures have occurred? What program has been carried forward in the state? The preceding chapters have constituted to a large degree the answers to these questions. It now remains to relate the answers into a unified whole, to interpret values, and to suggest certain desirable future steps in the program. This chapter is an attempt to unify the factors of the whole teacher-education situation in New Hampshire.

The type of educational control which has prevailed in New Hampshire, with the large amount of administrative freedom given to executive officers and their assistants, seems, on theoretical grounds, to favor the development of teacher-education programs, policies, and procedures. One fact stands out conspicuously: it has been possible and it has been the practice to get the facts in every instance, as Morrison did, beginning in 1904-1906 and later, and as Butterfield continued to do, and then, in the light of the data thus secured, to proceed to the adoption of such policies as seemed desirable in the light of all the facts.

CONSISTENT ADVANCEMENT OF GOALS
OF TEACHER EDUCATION

One exceedingly important fact about the whole plan of teacher-education in New Hampshire has been the possibility of moving up certification requirements consistently step by step, without the necessity of going to the legislature for authority, as fast as teachers with increasingly higher qualifications could be provided for the vacancies which occurred annually in the public-school system. It has been possible, also, to lengthen curricula of normal schools from time to time along with the advance in certification requirements, and otherwise to establish higher requirements for entrance to state normal schools and graduation from those institutions as teachers with better qualifications could be supplied to the state. It has been necessary at all times to keep the state supplied with teachers of the highest qualifications which could be secured at any one period and at the same time to furnish enough teachers to meet the demands made upon the normal schools. Under this plan standards have been advanced in a manner which has not been possible in states in which teacher certification has been governed by rigid statutory requirements instead of being placed in the hands of a policy-making board with an educator as executive officer and administrator.

Under the new state board of education, requirements for certification of teachers were established directly after the passage of the new education law in 1919. These requirements have been revised from time to time as seemed to be desirable in view of the facts. Revisions have progressively advanced the requirements for teaching in the state. They have ensured better and better teachers. At the same time, revisions and extensions of the curricula of state normal schools have been made.

The aim at the beginning of Morrison's administration was to make normal schools the instruments by which to place an educated and professionally prepared teacher in every elementary schoolroom in the state. Later that ideal included filling junior-high-school vacancies with normal-school graduates. Finally it seemed desirable to supply normal-school graduates for both academic and practical-arts work in secondary schools. Beginning in 1934, the goal has become that of furnishing for all elementary-school vacancies teachers with three years of professional preparation beyond a four-year secondary-school curriculum. In one or two years, as soon as the state is adjusted to the present requirements, the standard for elementary schools may be pushed forward to require a teacher with four years of professional preparation beyond high school as the minimum level of preparation. A four-year curriculum for elementary-school teachers has recently been introduced and it will doubtless soon become the minimum curriculum. The goal now includes preparation for every teacher in the secondary schools in a completely professionalized curriculum at least four years in length. This aim was established in Butterfield's administration and considerable progress toward its accomplishment already has been made. There are no side entrances to teaching in New Hampshire. Every teacher must be certificated by the state education department, and those who are not graduates of a New Hampshire institution must submit to an examination in addition to graduation from an accredited institution. This New Hampshire experience is thus a good example of long-time planning on the basis of a definite goal, and steady and consistent progress toward its ultimate accomplishment.

ADJUSTABLE CERTIFICATION REQUIREMENTS WITHOUT STATUTORY RESTRICTIONS

No limitations are placed upon the state board of education in requiring increasingly higher qualifications for teachers as rapidly as the needs of the schools can be supplied. This situation is in striking contrast to the difficulties which have been encountered in many states in which elaborate certification requirements have been made a part of the statutes. A comparison of certification requirements for any given type of teachers for two different periods a decade apart in New Hampshire reveals the progress which has been made. In the two statements which follow, the certification requirements for elementary-school teachers on two different dates, ten years apart, are given in order that the advance in these requirements may be clearly seen.

EXAMPLE OF EARLY CERTIFICATION REQUIREMENTS

The requirements which were in effect on September 1, 1924, were as follows for elementary-school teachers:

1. Teachers' certificates of elementary grade will be granted to candidates who are graduates of a New Hampshire normal school and present evidence of one year of successful teaching in New Hampshire.

2. Teachers' certificates of elementary grade will be granted to candidates who are graduates of an approved normal school of another state and who:
   (a) present satisfactory evidence of two years of successful teaching in New Hampshire, and
   (b) pass satisfactory examinations in the New Hampshire elementary program of studies and New Hampshire school law.

3. Teachers' certificates of elementary grade will be granted to graduates of high schools, who
   (a) present satisfactory evidence of four years of successful teaching in New Hampshire, and
   (b) pass satisfactory examinations in pedagogy and psychology, school management, New Hampshire elementary program and New Hampshire school law. Graduates of approved New Hampshire training schools may be granted elementary certificates upon presenting satisfactory evidence of two years' successful teaching in New Hampshire and passing the above examinations.[1]

EXAMPLE OF PRESENT CERTIFICATION REQUIREMENTS

In contrast with the foregoing requirements governing the certification of elementary-school teachers, another set of requirements is presented. They represent a decade of development, with no legislation of any kind. The requirements have been adjusted from time to time and new provisions added as fast as circumstances made possible further progress. The requirements of 1934 are here presented:

[1] Butterfield, E. W. "Rules and Regulations." *Report of the State Board of Education*, pp. 41-42. 1922.

1. New Hampshire normal school graduates in the elementary curricula will be given elementary licenses and at the close of one year of successful experience, following graduation, provided they have successfully passed examination in New Hampshire School Law and State Program of Studies, will receive elementary certificates.

2. Graduates of three-year elementary curricula in standard public normal schools in other states will be given elementary licenses renewable for two one-year periods. They must pass elementary examinations in Law and Program prior to September 1 of the year after service is begun. When they have taught two years with success in New Hampshire, they will receive Grade A elementary certificates. Graduates of elementary curricula in accredited normal schools in other states, which are less than three years in length, will not be eligible to begin service after July 1, 1935.

3. Graduates of two-year curricula in New Hampshire training schools prior to July 1, 1934, will be given elementary licenses renewable for one-year period. When they have taught one year with success in New Hampshire and have passed all state examinations, they will receive elementary certificates. Two years is permitted for the experience and the examination.

4. Graduates of three-year elementary curricula in standard private normal and training schools in other states will pass all the elementary examinations listed in the paragraphs under Examinations on page five. The examinations in Law and Program must be completed prior to September 1 of the year after service begins. Upon completion of the examinations and two years of experience, they will receive Grade A elementary certificates.

5 Graduates of elementary curricula in standard private normal and training schools in other states which are less than three years in length, will not be eligible to begin service after July 1, 1935.

6. Experienced elementary teachers with three or four years of successful service in the public schools of any state who register for summer training courses will be given licenses. They must take two full summer sessions in the New Hampshire normal schools and pass all examinations. When they have taught two years with success in New Hampshire and passed all state examinations, they will receive elementary certificates. Two years is [are] permitted for the experience and the examinations.

7. Experienced elementary teachers with five or more years of successful experience in the public schools of any state will be granted licenses which may be renewed for five years until the requirements for service certificates can be met.

8. In no case shall an applicant who begins service after July 1, 1934, be eligible under the provisions of sections 6 and 7 with less post-secondary training than that required for teachers in elementary schools by different sections of these regulations.

9. Candidates desiring to qualify under the provisions of sections 6 and 7 who have not been actively engaged in teaching for five or more years prior to applying for a credential will be granted licenses only upon evidence satisfactory to the State Board of Education that the candidates by study, by summer school courses or by other educational work are conversant with modern teaching practices and ideals.

The substantial advance in the requirements for elementary school teachers is evident in these regulations. It is not the fact of the advancement of the requirements during a given period that is most important. The significant fact is that the state board of education has power under the advice of the commissioner to establish new and higher requirements whenever the situation seems to warrant such action.

The principle of the progressive development of the requirements for teaching in New Hampshire is shown by a statement which Commissioner Butterfield made during the time that he was working on the problem and before a satisfactory solution had been reached. His comment shows the manner in which the requirements were built up in the face of an actual situation. He said:

In 1919, there were teaching in our state many who had never attended normal schools. In order that they might continue to qualify as teachers, these in considerable number for several years attended our summer sessions. With each year, teachers of this class have decreased in number.

To secure teachers so that all schools could be kept open, while the normal schools were developed, high-school graduates were for several years accepted as teachers. Two summer sessions were at first required parallel to the teaching. After two years this requirement was raised to four summer sessions and normal school credit was given toward graduation. In 1933, 108 entered the profession by this apprentice method and in 1924, 122 entered. . . . In 1925 the number of normal-school graduates had increased so that this class was limited to 25 and but 22 entered.

In 1926 the State Board was able to discontinue this plan, since trained teachers were available for all schools.[2]

All these facts indicate that normal-school curricula and requirements for certification of teachers in New Hampshire have remained stable, but at the same time progressive. Curricula and certification have gone ahead consistently under a single objective, namely, to give the state at all times a sufficient number of teachers with the highest possible qualifications.

CONTINUITY IN STATE EDUCATION OFFICE AND CONSISTENT PROGRESS IN TEACHER EDUCATION

Continuity of service in the office of state superintendent and commissioner of education have greatly favored the attainment of objectives in teacher education. Butterfield, who succeeded Morrison as state superintendent and who later became commissioner

[2] Butterfield, E. W. *Report of the State Board of Education*, pp. 129-130. 1926.

of education, had been a member of the state education department for a number of years. Likewise, Butterfield's successor as commissioner of education had been deputy commissioner of education throughout Butterfield's term as commissioner. Under these conditions there has been no break in the policy of the state for thirty years.

In the last three decades it has been unnecessary to consider political consequences to as great a degree as in many states. The state superintendent and the commissioner have had indefinite tenure, and the absence of hampering political conditions which would have restricted their freedom of action has characterized both their administrations. With Morrison and Butterfield no political considerations weighed in influencing their thinking or in determining action. No political opportunism on the part of presidents or local board members has been possible under the type of control that has existed. It has not been necessary for the commissioner to seek re-election every two or four years. The board has not been under the necessity of considering reappointments of staff. All the energies of the state education department could be devoted, therefore, to the study, formulation, and execution of educational policies. This freedom from politics for more than a quarter of a century has been one of the unique features of educational development in New Hampshire.

DIVISION OF SERVICE BETWEEN NORMAL SCHOOLS OF THE STATE

A very desirable division of service between the two normal schools has been organized. Both schools offer the three-year curriculum for elementary-school teachers, and preparation for junior-high-school teachers for both general and special subjects. The demand seems to require this at the present time. One normal school offers a four-year curriculum for high-school teachers of history which includes preparation for teaching various other high-school subjects as second teaching fields. Another normal school offers a four-year curriculum for high-school teachers of English with the same provisions with reference to second teaching fields. The second teaching fields may include, to the extent that it seems desirable, at least three years of work. Thus, junior-high-school and senior-high-school teachers are furnished in art, English, French, health and physical education, history, industrial arts, Latin, mathematics, music, natural science, and social science. Four-year curricula are offered in the normal schools, but not duplicated, in industrial arts, home economics, and commerce. The only teaching field in New Hampshire elementary and secondary schools for which provision is not made in the normal schools is that of agriculture. That, for the present, is reserved to the state university, which includes a college of agriculture.

The state is now almost in a position, and will be entirely in that position in a few years, to accomplish complete fulfillment of Morrison's ideal, namely, to raise, educate, and prepare professionally all the teachers needed to fill all vacancies in the entire public-school system. Thus has a great ideal come to realization under a consistent policy which has been carried forward unwaveringly for a considerable period of years.

EQUALITY IN PREPARATION OF RURAL-SCHOOL TEACHERS

The demand for equality in the preparation of rural-school teachers and teachers for village and city schools was especially stressed after 1919. On his appointment as commissioner, Butterfield accepted this task as one of the goals of teacher education in the state. Eleven years later this was written concerning it:

> In the years before 1919, it was held that the minimum education and training for teachers was for rural schools twelve years, for village and city schools fourteen years and for high schools sixteen years. Since 1919, we have decided that city and rural school children require and deserve teachers of equal education and equal training. The time is not far distant in this and other states when we shall agree that children of all ages and grades require and deserve teachers of equal maturity, cultural background and skilled preparation. This means four-year curricula for all prospective teachers, curricula differing for elementary and secondary teachers in content but not in extent nor in value.[3]

This well expresses the principle which previously has been discussed, namely: that a state, when it determines that it will, can put one-room rural schools first in teacher preparation. It was decided in New Hampshire, many years ago, that educational opportunities would be equalized for children throughout the state.[4] It only needed interest in equalizing opportunities for rural-school children, determination to equalize, and consistent effort toward that objective continued over a period of years with a state education department fully in control of the educational situation in the state.

[3] Butterfield, E. W. *Report of the State Board of Education*, p. 153. 1930.
[4] Morrison, Henry C. *Report of the State Superintendent of Public Instruction*, pp. 245-246. 1906.

EQUALIZATION OF EDUCATIONAL OPPORTUNITY THROUGH
TEACHER PREPARATION

Another form of equalization of educational opportunity has
gone forward in New Hampshire—that related to teachers of the
so-called practical-arts subjects. Time was when technicians with
some skill but limited education were the best who could be secured
as teachers of industrial arts. Teachers of commercial subjects oc-
casionally were college graduates with a year's additional work in
a business college, but more often they were persons of quite limited education who had acquired some skill in stenography and
typewriting and some proficiency in bookkeeping. Home economics
teachers were often persons of little education, but with some technical skill in cooking and sewing. New Hampshire pushed forward
the certification requirements and the preparation of such teachers
until, at the present time, all teachers in these fields must have had
specific professional preparation in a curriculum devoted primarily
to teacher education in one of these fields.

This progress is well summarized in the following statement,
which shows how requirements have been pushed forward consistently as fast as qualified teachers could be furnished in sufficient
numbers to fill all vacancies. Commissioner Butterfield, in 1930,
summarized the matter thus:

Qualified teachers in sufficient numbers are now available for home economics. They are trained so that in the smaller schools the teacher in addition to the domestic science of grades vii and viii and the home economics of
the senior high school may teach other high school classes as time permits.

In 1926, the State Board of Education enlarged its three-year domestic
arts curriculum at the Keene Normal School to a four-year home economics
curriculum and its graduates readily find employment and are teaching with
success. The state university also prepares home economics teachers for
our schools.

For many years the usual teachers of commerce in our high schools were
young persons whose period of preparation was inferior to the high school
standards for teachers of other subjects. The requirement was office practice
and a year in a business college or technical school. These teachers could
bring to their work no broad view or native culture and as a result the
commerce department in our high schools was in poor repute.

This situation was manifestly an undesirable one. Equality of educational
opportunities does not mean that students of Latin shall be well taught
while students of stenography shall have inferior teachers, nor does the
welfare of the state permit such a distinction. Accordingly the state standard for teachers of commerce has been repeatedly raised. First, two

years of training; then, three years; and now a requirement of four years of training as for high school teachers of other subjects. There are some who think that all college graduates may teach Latin, history and mathematics but, fortunately, there are none who think that the same college graduate may teach stenography, typewriting, and bookkeeping. This made it a necessity that the state train its own teachers and, in 1916, at the normal schools were established three-year curricula in commerce. In 1926, the work was assigned to the Plymouth Normal School with a full four-year curriculum leading to the degree of Bachelor of Education. Specific training for high school teachers of commerce is not now given, nor has it been, at any other institution in the state.

Until recently we have had few teachers available with education and training sufficient for full high school work in mechanic arts. The situation is now changed. In 1926, the State Board of Education extended its three-year manual training curriculum at the Keene Normal School to a four-year mechanic arts curriculum and its graduates are now teaching in our city mechanic arts courses. We propose, as the need continues, to give also the specialized training necessary for teachers who will be able to develop this work in the smaller high schools.

. . . The mechanic arts and home economics curricula at the Keene Normal School are approved by the Federal Board for Vocational Education and the maintenance cost of their extension to four-year courses is balanced by federal subsidies.[5]

SUCCESS IN FURNISHING NORMAL-SCHOOL GRADUATES FOR ALL TYPES OF SCHOOLS

New Hampshire did not begin the preparation of high-school teachers in its normal schools until it had accomplished its objective of service to the rural schools. State normal schools have often been criticized for neglecting the preparation of rural school teachers. Some of the criticism has been pertinent. It is an exceedingly significant fact that in 1928-1929, of 142 vacancies in one-room rural schools, 140 were filled with normal-school graduates who had had two years of professional preparation beyond secondary-school graduation. Likewise, of 116 vacancies in village schools 104 were filled with normal-school graduates. Furthermore, 18 of 23 vacancies in city schools and 48 of 113 in high schools were similarly filled.[6] Thus practically all vacancies in elementary schools and nearly one-half the vacancies in secondary schools were filled with graduates of New Hampshire normal schools. Two years before that 130 of 132 vacancies in one-room rural schools were filled with normal-school graduates, 98 of 105 village-school vacancies, and

[5] Butterfield, E. W. *Report of the State Board of Education*, pp. 121-122. 1930.
[6] *Ibid.*, p. 78.

33 of 42 city-school vacancies. In the same year 32 of 109 high-school vacancies were filled by New Hampshire normal-school graduates.[7] The rapid gain in filling high-school vacancies with normal-school graduates supports the statement that it will soon be possible to fill all such vacancies from that source. The normal-school graduates who teach in high schools teach both academic and practical-arts subjects. These figures do not include a considerable number of normal-school graduates who have had departmental work in six-year high schools and whose work is mostly in the seventh and eighth grades but who have upper classes in some subjects.[8] It is said that:

> The demand for these graduates in the high schools of the state is increasing and is each year greater than the supply.[9]

A PERMANENT TEACHING STAFF BY PREPARATION OF NATIVE STOCK

The annual overturn in the teaching staff, even in 1928, caused considerable concern as it had all through the earlier years. Butterfield, in that year, said:

> An annual overturn of 388 in a total of 2993 is disastrous to good work. If all of our elementary and high school teachers were trained in our normal schools, this loss could be reduced to 300. It can be seen that the least stability is among rural and high school teachers.[10]

The principle upon which it was believed that it would be possible to secure a permanent teaching staff for the secondary schools of the state was reiterated many times in the state education reports. It seemed to be a fact that a teaching staff drawn from institutions located a long distance away would be inferior, generally, to a staff native to the state, whether they were prepared in outside institutions or in those located within the state. Persons from the best native stock could not be secured for teachers, it was believed, under these conditions. This principle was clearly expressed again in 1928 in the following language:

> The overturn is large among high school teachers. Vacancies are usually filled by untrained graduates from institutions in other states. Their interest in New Hampshire is small, and, if they succeed, they seek schools nearer home or at least in larger cities than those in New Hampshire . . . *We need for permanent teachers in all our schools New Hampshire girls trained in New Hampshire normal schools.*[11]

[7] Butterfield, E. W. *Report of the State Board of Education*, p. 76. 1928.
[8] *Ibid.*, p. 76.   [9] *Ibid.*, p. 76.
[10] *Ibid.*, p. 77.   [11] *Ibid.*, p. 77.

TWO FACTORS IN DEVELOPING A PERMANENT TEACHING STAFF

Two factors undoubtedly had a great deal of effect on developing a permanent teaching staff for New Hampshire schools, especially in inducing young women to go to one-room country schools and to small country high schools. (a) In the first place secondary-school development in New Hampshire has tended toward the establishment of small high schools in somewhat remote rural communities. The law which has required those communities not maintaining high schools to pay tuition of pupils in other high schools in the state has often stimulated these small communities to use their funds to establish a high school in their own community. Since the secondary schools of the state have been under a rigid state control which could assure well-prepared teachers, proper equipment and suitable buildings, and a degree of excellence comparable to that in secondary schools in larger places, it was possible for a good many communities to maintain a small but standard secondary school. The outlet for girls especially, in such communities, was limited as compared with the opportunities in commercial employment in the larger cities. Thus these young women were willing to teach in country schools, and that often furnished the only opportunity for employment. By this means, young women who represented strong native stock went to the normal schools, and many of them came back, not necessarily to their home towns, but to the general region, to serve as teachers in the schools. (b) In the second place, the practice of requiring a large number of the graduating classes of the normal schools in the elementary-school curriculum to do nine weeks of student teaching in one-room rural schools was a large factor in inducing normal-school graduates to accept positions in country schools. These young women were graduates of high schools located in rural communities, and, after nine weeks of student-teaching in a rural school, they were willing to go back to such schools to be teachers. These factors have been important influences in placing in the New Hampshire rural schools a staff of teachers which in a few years will consist almost entirely of normal-school graduates, all new teachers in such schools being equipped with four years of professional preparation. Three years of preparation are now required and an optional four-year curriculum has been introduced. It is assumed that in the near future four years of professional education will be the minimum requirement.

TWO SIGNIFICANT ERAS IN TEACHER EDUCATION

Between 1904 and 1934 two eras in teacher education in the state seemed to have been completed. The end of Morrison's administration marked the termination of one era. At that time, certain fundamental teacher-education policies had been established in the state and the normal-school program had been reorganized along modern lines as conceived in that period. The situation had been brought into a state of readiness for the further reorganization of administrative control and the development in policies which took place under Commissioner Butterfield. At the end of Butterfield's term in 1930, when he responded to a call to the commissionership in a neighboring state, another era had reached its consummation. The plan of teacher education and certification current at that time had been brought to substantial completion. The normal schools were then operating consistently under the centralized type of control which had been established and they had entered upon teachers-college status. Physical plants and training-school facilities had been developed to the point of adequacy for the current enrollments. All this seemed to mark the end of another era.

Under their present policy of centralized control and unification the normal schools of the state now seem ready to proceed into another era of development and to go forward along new lines different from those of either of the past two periods. Perhaps few states, if any, are as ready as is New Hampshire for certain next steps in teacher education which need to be taken in this country.

CHAPTER XIII

PRESENT VALUES IN TEACHER EDUCATION IN NEW HAMPSHIRE

THIS chapter constitutes an attempt to estimate some values in the current policies and program of teacher education in New Hampshire. The course of historical development of the education of teachers in New Hampshire has been traced in some detail from the earliest beginnings. The current status of teacher education in the state has been described and discussed. These presentations furnish a basis for considering some of the issues raised at the beginning. Certain questions were proposed in Chapter I. It is possible to discuss interpretatively some of those questions on the basis of the data which have been presented.

MODERN SECONDARY SCHOOL MADE POSSIBLE BY PREVAILING TYPE OF TEACHER EDUCATION

The modern secondary school as it now exists in New Hampshire was made possible by the type of teacher preparation which has prevailed in the state. At the beginning of his administration, Morrison began a development of secondary schools in New Hampshire which represented the state university idea applied to the secondary-school level. He began at the outset to develop diversified offerings in the high schools and academies of the state. This program did not go forward on the basis of a wide range of electives which pupils might choose, but it proceeded by setting up a number of distinct curricula each four years in length and each constructed around a continuous and well-organized sequence of four years of work in some field which was suitable as a basis for secondary education. Thus, unified four-year curricula appeared in the high schools and academies in commerce, mechanic arts, household arts, and agriculture. These curricula were not essentially vocational but were primarily educational. The work of these curricula was thought of as contributing to the general education of the individual, and it was not organized primarily for the purpose of vocational training.   Students were not permitted to take small amounts of different subjects and thus attain graduation by the mere accumulation of credits.   They were required to pursue some one of these fields through a prescribed sequence of courses extending from the beginning to the end of the secondary-school period.   Some of these studies began in the junior high school.

At the outset, teachers were not available for this new type of secondary-school work.   Liberal-arts colleges did not prepare teachers for those fields.   Normal schools in New Hampshire did not furnish a sufficient number of such teachers.   These curricula in high schools did not become educationally successful until a generation of teachers had been prepared who understood the educational possibilities of these practical-arts subjects in secondary schools. Thus, it can be said that the normal schools of New Hampshire made possible the modern expanded secondary school which now prevails in that state.   They made possible the teaching of industrial arts, household arts, and commerce from an educational point of view.   It is clearly evident that in the last decade and a half the unified and centralized type of educational control in the state greatly favored the development of secondary education of this broader and more significant kind by the very fact that a type of teacher education best adapted to its consummation had been created.

MIGRATION OF TEACHERS UNCHECKED BY TEACHER-EDUCATION POLICY

It is apparent that the teacher-education policy which was carried forward for a quarter of a century has not enabled the state to hold its teachers.   The annual exodus seems to continue unabated.   It is impossible to state how many more teachers might have been lost to the state had not past and present policies prevailed.   Possibly a large migration of teachers from New Hampshire is inevitable under any conditions.   Study of all influences which might prevent migration of teachers is indicated as a desirable future policy.

It seems clear that other influences in addition to preparation of native stock for teachers for New Hampshire schools will be necessary to prevent the present great annual exodus of teachers.   New Hampshire girls in large numbers will always leave New Hampshire schools to accept positions in Massachusetts and Connecticut as long as higher salaries prevail in those states.   It may be that the absence of a good teacher's retirement law is a factor in New Hampshire's inability to hold its teachers. Possibly the remoteness of some parts of the state from centers of population may have some influence. In any case, the policy of the state during the last two decades to encourage young men and women of the state to prepare for teaching and to remain in the state as teachers is wise and commendable. Recent efforts to encourage girls in rural communities to prepare for teaching and then return to teach in the rural schools seems like a sound policy. It seems clear that both Morrison and Butterfield sensed a most important danger to the state in this particular and did all that could be done to build counteracting influences.

New Hampshire needs to supplement these efforts by such additional encouragement to teachers as higher salaries and an adequate retirement law. Evidence is not at hand, of course, to indicate that these changes would immediately check the migration of teachers to other states. These improvements are merely suggested as a part of a plan to surround teachers with such favorable conditions that they will be more willing to remain for longer periods in the communities in which they teach.

THE REAL BASIS FOR A STABLE TEACHING STAFF

Morrison has suggested one possible solution for this problem. He advocates that states abolish their corporate districts and administer their school systems as branches of their respective civil services, transferring teachers from contractual status to civil service and setting up teacher-preparation service just adequate to supply the necessary recruitment.[1] He further points out certain consequences which he believes would follow. Unprepared teachers would soon disappear. Teachers might be placed where they were needed without reference to the ability of any given district to pay. Educational opportunities so far as good teaching is concerned could be equalized, for the best teachers could not congregate where economic conditions were best. Salary schedules would tend to be the same throughout the state and throughout the nation if such a plan were generally adopted, and teachers would receive equivalent pay regardless of where they were sent. Morrison points out that at the present time salaries of teachers are

. . . determined by the law of wages in an economic field in which there is no natural commodity-price control of competition.[2]

[1] Morrison, Henry C. "Economics of Personal Service." *The Management of the School Money*, p. 233-234.   [2] *Ibid.*, p. 234.

It would be possible, he concludes, to make certain adjustments for differences in the cost of living so that the base salaries would represent the true salary income.[3]

This is a fundamental principle, which departs far from current practice and most contemporary thinking. No state in the country has yet chosen this organization. Morrison contends that no good reason exists, however, why states should not begin to adopt such a plan or why, under such plans, teaching service should not be equally remunerated in all parts of the country. It is doubtful that professionally educated teachers comparable to professional workers in other professions can be furnished in the several states until basic policies are adopted which accord with sound economics of personal service in the area of social service. It seems certain, however, that even such sound and effective policies as Morrison and Butterfield established for producing a stable teaching staff in New Hampshire, will never solve the problem. Something else is needed.

Another point of view with reference to the financing of education which is quite opposed to that held by Morrison, must be given consideration in this connection. The proponents[4] of this view hold that educational opportunity and the cost of its support should be equalized up to a reasonably satisfactory minimum and the cost of such equalization borne by state funds. They believe that by furnishing this minimum program on the basis of state support, local initiative can be made possible by releasing local tax resources for the purpose of enriching and extending the foundation program. Will it not be likely, however, that under such a plan some communities will be able to enrich the program and some will not? Will not educational opportunities thus fail to be equalized? Will not some communities have teachers with minimum salaries and minimum preparation, while others will offer higher salaries and seek and obtain more superior teachers? Under Morrison's theory the procedure recommended by the National Conference on the Financing of Education would retain all the evils of the inter-district competitive system which he deplores. The best teachers would then congregate in those places which were willing to tax themselves in order to secure for their children superior educational opportunities. According to Morrison, salaries would thus be determined by a law

[3] *Ibid.*, p. 234.
[4] See, for example, Norton, John K., and Others. *Report of National Conference on the Financing of Education*, pp. 13-14, 1933.

of wages which has no commodity-price control of competition.[5]   A better plan, he thinks, would be to have teachers' salaries determined by standards of merit and service without dependence on local ability or willingness to pay.   Morrison's analysis in the economics of personal service leads one inevitably to the conclusion that proponents of the opposing view here discussed neglect to consider defensible economic principles which relate to the purchase of teaching service.   This view of the problem does not necessarily contemplate creation of a series of maxima beyond which education cannot develop.   It does, however, seek a basis for teachers' salaries in sound economics of personal service in the field of social service. The real question for consideration here is: Which of these two plans is the better calculated to produce a stable teaching staff in which educational opportunities for children will be equalized as nearly as possible?   Morrison's entire statement follows:

Each of the states must organize its teacher-training forces on a noncompetitive basis, admit to training annually the number of persons which is sufficient to meet the recruitment and no more, refuse to permit any but trained teachers in the public schools, and extend the training required in point of time and in point of severity as rapidly as the accumulation of scientific material may make possible.

If the conditions under which the State competes with itself, as well in the training colleges as in the districts, are thus removed, the recruitment required, interacting with the training imposed and checked by the limitations of taxation, must in due season produce a teaching force of career people operating at the economic level which is objectively compatible with professional requirements and compatible with the economic condition of low risk under which teachers operate.   Beyond that point incomes in teaching and other socialized services move upward only as the general standard of living, based on amount and distribution of popular income, itself moves upward.[6]

It is impossible to reach any final conclusion on the controversial issue raised by these two opposing points of view.   It is within the province of this study, however, to suggest that some plan needs to be adopted by which greater stability may be introduced into the teaching staff of the state of New Hampshire in order to remove certain deplorable consequences which result from the present amount of change in the teaching personnel.   Perhaps the final conclusion can be reached only when these and other plans are tried in practice and subjected to experimental evaluation.

[5] Morrison, Henry C. Op. cit., p. 234.
[6] Ibid., p. 257.

ELEMENTS OF UNIQUENESS IN NEW HAMPSHIRE PLAN FOR METHODOLOGICAL STUDY OF SUBJECT MATTER

Morrison's plan for methodological study of subject matter has been considered in a previous chapter. It was, and still remains, a basic procedure in the New Hampshire normal schools. Butterfield recognized merit in the idea and carried forward the conception and the practice with still further refinement. Students now, prevailingly, begin with the study of the materials of the elementary- or secondary-school curriculum and go backward into such advanced materials as are deemed necessary as a basis for teaching content in some teaching field.

The introduction of this plan of teacher education in the two New Hampshire normal schools raised one important question: Can the normal school begin at the outset to study the process of organizing appropriate materials of pupil education without previous extended academic study as a background for such content? In the New Hampshire normal schools under Morrison's reorganization, the subject matter of the traditional elementary-school subjects was directly approached as professional study of the materials of pupil education. Even though courses were offered in each of the several subjects of the elementary school, he did not conceive of it wholly by subjects. It was not compartmentalized to the degree that sometimes has characterized later curricula of normal schools and teachers colleges. Under such heads as "pedagogy" and "psychology of primary subjects," terms found in Morrison's original draft of the curriculum,[7] a direct and unified attack upon the professional treatment of the materials of the elementary school was begun and pushed forward to completion in close relation to both the theory of teaching and student teaching. The unification of the study of the materials of the elementary program in a few courses saved time for more participation and more study of subjects like music and art in which students were less proficient than in traditional subjects.

SIGNIFICANT QUESTION RAISED BY THE NEW HAMPSHIRE EXPERIENCE

This experience in New Hampshire raised a second question, which is still unanswered: What amount of purely academic study,

---

[7] Morrison, Henry C. "Reorganization of the Normal Schools." *Report of the Superintendent of Public Instruction*, pp. 204-205. 1916.

apart from work needed as a general cultural background, is desirable in those fields in which the student expects to teach? Three years' consideration of curriculum materials and study of academic background in the case of teaching subjects like history or Latin or French is the amount required in New Hampshire. If this proves to be a sufficient amount of study in a teaching field to provide an adequate grasp of curriculum materials and a sufficient background for these materials for teaching purposes in any field, it opens the way for the introduction of a large amount of more general cultural-foundation study. This cultural-foundation study is believed by many people to be a very desirable element in the teachers-college curriculum.

The question may be stated in another way: Is it possible to place students at the outset in a training-school situation in which they are confronted with the need for subject matter in the actual guidance of children and in which they will study only so much subject matter as that situation requires? By beginning with observation and the very simplest situations student teachers would gradually gain ability in creating subject matter as they slowly advance into more and more responsible teaching over a period of years. Or, again: Is it possible for students to begin with the guidance of children in simple situations involving at first little responsibility, to find there the problem of the need for subject matter, to follow the leads created in these contacts with children, and to work toward such background of subject matter as is needed until they have reached whatever attainment in that direction seems to be desirable for teaching purposes?

FOUR PROCEDURES IN THE SUBJECT-MATTER PREPARATION OF TEACHERS

No practical way to measure the success of teachers several years after graduation is now available, so that the graduates of different normal schools may be compared and the different plans for preparing teachers be evaluated.[8] It is certainly impossible to say, from the viewpoint of measured results, that this approach to subject matter which has been described is better than some other. It is not possible, therefore, to make any conclusive statements concerning the results of the preparation which teachers receive in New Hamp-

[8] "The Education of Teachers Evaluated through Measurement of Teaching Ability." *National Survey of the Education of Teachers*, 5:87-153. 1933.

shire except on the basis of principles of teacher education which are now generally accepted as sound by students of the field. Measured by that criterion, this experience in New Hampshire seems to conform to what many competent students would call good practice. It demonstrated four procedures in the education of teachers so far as subject matter is concerned: (*a*) intrinsic motivation of the learning of subject matter by student teachers in response to their own recognition of need for the materials of pupil education for use in actual teaching, at the beginning of the period of preparation; (*b*) large dependence upon responsible student teaching and the consequent extensive use of subject matter in teaching as an element in acquiring a wide control of the materials of pupil education and for studying advanced materials as a background for curriculum materials; (*c*) study of subject matter as the organization of children's materials progresses and shows need for background from which to constitute the materials of pupil learning; (*d*) extended contact, as necessary, with new subject matter in this methodological approach, in the fields in which students have had less experience in secondary and lower schools.

CONCEPTION OF THE TEACHERS COLLEGE AS A SMALL INSTITUTION

All the evidence points to the fact that Morrison found in his studies ample reasons, supported by his philosophy, for concluding that normal schools should be small institutions. This idea runs through the different biennial reports. In 1914, he suggested enrollments of 175, 300, 250, and 150 for four proposed normal schools. He stated at the same time that in one of the existing normal schools it was impossible to deal adequately with an enrollment of more than 100 students. He also stated in the same report that at the new state normal school in Keene, with the entire city elementary-school system available for training-school purposes, it would be possible adequately to prepare an enrollment of 300 students provided the state could make further contracts with school districts in other neighboring towns.[9] Again, in the biennial report of 1916 Morrison estimated the number who could be adequately prepared at Keene to be from 250 to 300 students. He further stated that an enrollment of 250 students at the normal school would adequately supply that area with professionally prepared teachers. He mentioned again the need of a normal school in the northern part of the

Ibid., p. 156.

state with an enrollment somewhat smaller than that of the school at Plymouth which then had about 175 students.[10] Morrison concluded, as he had on previous occasions, that an effective normal school must be located in a community which has a sufficiently large school system to offer opportunities for student teaching for an economically large number of students.[11] This means a normal school only large enough that the processes of teacher education may operate in a desirable manner.

Does this conception of the small normal school or teachers college offer a suggestion for the present situation throughout the country? Some states have established a small number of large teachers colleges. Others have maintained a larger number of small institutions. The suggestion for the future seems to lie in the direction of a sufficient number of small institutions located at convenient population centers throughout the state. The greatly reduced number of new teachers now annually required by public-school systems seems to point in this direction. In New Hampshire, in 1922, for example, 352 new elementary-school teachers were employed, while in 1934 only 125 such teachers were needed. The total need for teachers decreased from 477 in 1922 to 166 in 1934.[12]

In this connection, however, other factors must be taken into consideration. What are the conditions of supply and demand? What sources of supply other than normal schools are available? The facts concerning the annual number of new teachers needed in New Hampshire indicate a smaller demand than has prevailed in the past. The same situation seems to exist in other states. Is the United States not tending in the direction of some foreign countries in this particular? In the United States, it is estimated, 400,000 students are under preparation for teaching.[13] Germany has a population about half as great as that of the United States and it has only about 5,000 students preparing to be teachers. Various reasons account for the small number of such students in Germany, some of which do not apply, and will not at least for a long time, in America. Nevertheless, some conditions here point to far greater

[10] Morrison, Henry C. "Education and Training of Teachers." *Report of the Superintendent of Public Instruction*, p. 176. 1916.

[11] *Ibid.*, p. 176.

[12] Pringle, James N. *Report of the State Board of Education*, p. 55. 1934.

[13] Alexander, Thomas. "The Training of Teachers in Europe." *National Survey of the Education of Teachers*, 5:389. Washington, D. C.: United States Department of the Interior, Office of Education. 1935.

stability in the teaching staff than has prevailed in the past. The rapid decrease in the number of new teachers in New Hampshire, if the same conditions exist in the other states, may indicate a trend in this direction. Surely then the enrollment in university schools of education, and in normal schools and teachers colleges, especially in those which provide undergraduate preparation for the new teachers needed annually in the states, will be likely to decrease if states admit to preparation only the number of students required annually for recruiting the teaching staff.

It seems, on the basis of the evidence and this type of reasoning, that two small and adequately equipped normal schools, located in convenient population centers in New Hampshire, organized as branches of the state university and supplementary to it, would constitute adequate facilities to furnish all the teachers which the state needs. Each normal school would require several buildings, namely, one or more dormitories, one or more classroom buildings, and a training school. These buildings should be the very best of their type with suitable auditoriums, gymnasiums, classrooms, workrooms, libraries, and all other necessary facilities for preparing teachers. If the normal schools were located in sufficiently large communities, as one now is, it would be possible to supply the continuous experience in varied classroom contacts, now considered a part of the process of teacher education. Students could observe and teach for a period of time in an adequate campus training school and have an abundance of contacts with schools of different types in the community. Under one philosophy of teacher education which has considerable approval in this country abundant experience as a most significant aspect of learning can hardly be overestimated. The question may well be raised, then, whether the necessity for providing both extensive experience in teaching and realistic participation in a wide range of cultural living throughout the period of preparation does not limit teachers colleges in all states to relatively small enrollments. Probably the optimum enrollment will need to be determined experimentally.

From the point of view of expense and adequate teacher education, this idea seems to have a great deal to commend it. The prediction is made that as modern principles of teacher education become better and better established, states will find it most desirable to administer teacher education, like medical education, in relatively small institutions. States do not seem to hesitate to establish multimillion-dollar medical schools for a few carefully selected students. Why should not the same principle be applied to teacher education?

PROPOSAL TO UNITE NORMAL SCHOOLS IN SINGLE STATE-UNIVERSITY ORGANIZATION

By holding the enrollment of normal schools and teachers colleges at the limit determined by careful planning states are furnished with only the number of teachers that they need; thus they may secure a sufficiently economical administration of their teachers colleges to enable them to provide highly-prepared and well-paid faculties and all needed equipment and facilities for each institution. Perhaps all the teachers colleges of a state could be organized into one comprehensive institution known as the teachers college of the state. For example the teachers colleges of New Hampshire and the state university might well be united into a single state-university organization under one board. Such a plan would probably result in greater unity in the education of teachers. Undoubtedly greater effectiveness would result from the adoption of these principles.

NEED FOR PROGRAM OF SELECTIVE ADMISSION AND ELIMINATION

The selection of candidates for teacher education has been given considerable consideration in recent years. New Hampshire has not done a great deal as yet in limiting enrollments, for it has not needed to restrict attendance at the state normal schools. It is likely that the time has now come when a very rigid plan of selective admission and post-admission selection within the institutions should be adopted. Certain regulations are now in force which require applicants to rank well in the secondary schools which they attended and to come to the normal school for an interview before admission. It seems likely that further steps toward better selection should now be taken. No perfect plan for recruiting the most superior type of material among high-school graduates for teacher education has yet been developed. Many practices are in operation in different institutions apparently with varying degrees of success.[14]

It is beyond the scope of this study to enter into a detailed dis-

[14] Baker, Frank E. "Selective Admission and Selective Promotion in Teacher Educating Institutions." *Yearbook* No. *XXIII of the National Society of College Teachers of Education*, pp. 16-65. University of Chicago Press. 1935.

cussion of this problem or to suggest a plan for selective admission to New Hampshire teacher-education institutions. Two statements, however, may be made. First, it seems desirable to recruit for teacher education the very best material among the high-school graduates. Second, it is desirable to set up the best possible plan for restricting admission to normal schools and teachers colleges to the most superior graduates of secondary schools.

Then the question immediately arises: What is it that constitutes superiority in graduates of secondary schools, with reference to their suitability for teacher education? In the past and even at the present time intellectual superiority has seemed to be the main criterion. It now seems somewhat doubtful that as a single basis for judgment this is the most desirable criterion. What are the qualities and the characteristics which indicate pre-teacher-preparation suitability in a candidate? It is beyond the scope of this study to enter into a detailed discussion of this question or even to review the various investigations which have been made. Kriner has raised the question:

What qualities are needed for teacher success and which qualities can be recognized before the time, money, and energy of both the student and the teacher training institution have been spent in professional preparation?[15]

Butterfield has recently pointed out that not only is teaching an intellectual pursuit but it demands certain qualities which make it a social grace.[16] Certainly this viewpoint is justified under the conception of education which is rapidly emerging.

The absurdity of the present situation is evident when consideration is given to the conditions of mass preparation of teachers in most states at the present time far in excess of any reasonable needs. The more unified policy which is inevitable under the type of centralized authority which now exists in New Hampshire and which would be further extended by the adoption of these suggestions, would remedy a great many of the difficulties which now prevail in teacher education in that and other states. A new study of teacher demand and supply in New Hampshire is indicated.[17]

[15] Kriner, Harry L. *Pre-Training Factors Predictive of Teacher Success*, p. 7. Penn State Studies in Education, No. 1. State College, Pennsylvania. 1931.
[16] Butterfield, E. W. "Teaching as a Social Grace." *National Education Association—Proceedings of the Seventy-third Annual Meeting*, pp. 688-694. 1935.
[17] See Myers, Alonzo F. "Teacher Demand, Supply and Certification." *Yearbook No. XXIII of the National Society of College Teachers of Education*, pp. 186-209. University of Chicago Press. 1935.

UNIFICATION OF TEACHER EDUCATION DESIRABLE IN
NEW HAMPSHIRE

Among the teacher-education problems which still remain to be solved in New Hampshire, the unification of the agencies for teacher preparation is among the most important. New Hampshire is like most other states in this particular. Generally, a threefold division of energy is found in the preparation of teachers. Liberal-arts colleges under private control usually devote some part of their energies to teacher preparation. Nearly every state has a state university which maintains a school of education for the preparation of teachers. Almost every state has one or more state normal schools or state teachers colleges which are devoted wholly or in part to teacher education. Great inco-ordination usually exists among these three types of teacher-education institutions.

It may well be that the functions of teacher education in the normal schools and the University of New Hampshire have not been well adjusted. In the first place the normal schools and the department of education of the state university have until recently been under two separate boards and the present interlocking arrangement between these boards has not yet resolved the difficulties of disjunction. In the second place the curricula of the normal schools and that of the department of education of the state university are constructed on very different educational policies. Great differences also exist in the type of preparation given to high-school teachers in the state university and that which such teachers receive in the state normal schools. Thus there is a very evident lack of co-ordination and co-operative planning between the two institutions.

It has been pointed out recently that the division which formerly existed and which still persists between colleges and universities, on the one hand, and normal schools and teachers colleges, on the other, must be abolished.[18] The two types of institutions must be united so far as preparation of teachers is concerned.[19] This union is lacking in New Hampshire. The state normal schools are under the control of the state board of education and the direct supervision of the commissioner of education. The department of education of the university is under the trustees of that institution. Why not place both institutions under the trustees of the university?

[18] "Conclusions and Recommendations of the Commission," pp. 112-113. *Report of the Commission on Social Studies.* New York: Charles Scribner's Sons. 1934.
[19] *Ibid.*, p. 112.

PROPOSAL FOR UNIFICATION OF TEACHER EDUCATION IN NEW HAMPSHIRE

It is proposed, therefore, that all teacher education in New Hampshire be unified under one board. It is further proposed that a unified teacher-education policy for the undergraduate preparation of teachers be developed in the state normal schools and the University of New Hampshire under the immediate supervision of a state director of teacher education, who might be the dean of education in the proposed state-university organization in which it is recommended that the normal schools be included.

GRADUATE PREPARATION IN EDUCATION IN NEW HAMPSHIRE

The question of a graduate school for advanced preparation of teachers and superintendents is an important problem for every state to consider at the present time. Many high schools now require, or at least seek, one or more years of graduate study for their teachers. Under present conditions it is possible to secure for high school work and in limited numbers even for elementary schools, teachers who hold the master's degree. Persons holding the doctor's degree are beginning to find their way into high schools. This is desirable provided the degree represents broad preparation in cultural fields, essential understandings in teaching content, and a comprehension of the educative process and the means by which growth and development take place in school pupils. It is predicted that an increasingly large number of promising young men and women with advanced preparation will become available for high-school teaching and, eventually, it is hoped, for teaching in elementary schools.

New Hampshire should have a strong graduate school of education. Graduate study in education today needs to be maintained on a very high professional level, comparable in every particular with graduate professional work in other fields. It seems desirable, then, that a strong graduate school of education be maintained at the University of New Hampshire. It should offer an extensive program for the adequate and proper preparation of principals and superintendents who need study which would lead to the doctor's degree in education including the fields of psychology, educational administration, philosophy of education, theory and principles of teaching, curriculum construction, comparative education, history of education, and educational economics. Such work should be supplemented by broadly conceived academic study in the fields of economics, political science, government, sociology, anthropology, history, fine arts, and science. The object should be not merely the technical equipment of educators, but the preparation of men and women to become constructive leaders in their communities. No less preparation than that leading to the doctor's degree should be accepted in the case of principals, supervisors, and superintendents.

The proposed university graduate school of education should have a small but highly qualified faculty and appropriate courses leading to the degrees of master of education and doctor of education. The doctor's degree should not be essentially a research degree. The number of courses needed for these purposes need not be as large as is often contemplated. Many of the present narrow compartmentalized subjects may be integrated into a relatively few broad fields of study in comprehensive year courses or even two-year courses, in each of which several professors and a relatively small group of students will together study and discuss the various problems with which the courses deal.

Elementary school teachers should be encouraged to take advanced work beyond the bachelor's degree. Both elementary and secondary experimental schools should be maintained in connection with the school of education, but not for practice-teaching purposes. New curriculum materials should be in constant process of formulation both at the state university and at the normal schools. Other experiments should be carried on at both types of institutions. The school of education of the state university should be an independent unit under its own dean.

FINAL ESTIMATE OF VALUES IN TEACHER EDUCATION

This chapter has attempted to interpret values, to estimate progress, to discover failures and their causes, and to consider critically some important aspects of the policies and the program in teacher education which have been developed in New Hampshire. It has been difficult to differentiate between progress which has come as the effect of the personalities and the leadership of two very outstanding commissioners of education and advancement which has resulted from the centralized type of state control and administration of education including teacher preparation which has prevailed in New Hampshire. Perhaps the two factors happening together have been most fortunate. It seems to be a justifiable conclusion that the progress during the last fifteen years would not have been so great in the absence of the centralized type of administration. The evidence seems to point to many factors under the new plan inaugurated in 1919 which the commissioner of education used to the advantage of teacher education and for which no substitute would have been available under a decentralized type of administration. It is necessary, then, to conclude that while the personalities and the leadership of the two commissioners who held that office from 1904 to 1930, were strong factors in the development of teacher education in New Hampshire, the one would have accomplished even more than he did if he had had at his command the more centralized type of administration which later prevailed; and the other would have been greatly hindered without the centralized control which he was able to utilize to the fullest extent in the interests of the policies and the program of teacher education which he developed in the state.

It should be pointed out that although a high degree of centralized control resided in the state office of education, local initiative and freedom in administration and in formulating and adopting institutional policies prevailed in the normal schools to as great a degree as would have been desirable under complete decentralization.

The continuity in office and the character and the non-political attitude of the members of the state board of education, together with their great interest in the educational welfare of the state, were powerful factors in the whole situation. Credit needs to be accorded the various governors who have appointed and reappointed the members of the state board of education and who have thus continued in office members who had rendered good service without regard to their political affiliation. These conditions offered the opportunity to create teacher-education policies, to modify them as seemed necessary, and to continue them in operation over a long period of years so that they could be tested and adjusted from time to time under the same administration and be moved forward constantly to ever greater perfection. The fact that a form of state school administration existed which made this possible and the fact that two state administrators of education created these conditions and used their fullest potentialities for the benefit of teacher education represent the greatest and most significant values in teacher education in New Hampshire. This perhaps best condenses into a single statement the essential values in teacher education in New Hampshire.

BIBLIOGRAPHY

Bagley, William C. *Significant Trends in Teacher Training.* Unpublished Address Delivered at the Seventy-fifth Anniversary of the Founding of the State Normal School at Salem, Massachusetts. September 19, 1929.

Barnard, Henry. *Normal Schools and Other Institutions, Agencies, and Means Designed for the Professional Education of Teachers: Part I. United States and Provinces,* p. 157.

Barstow, George. *The History of New Hampshire from Its Discovery in 1614 to the Passage of the Toleration Act in 1819.* Concord: State Library.

Beard, Charles A. and Others. "Conclusions and Recommendations of the Commission." *Report of the Commission on Social Studies.* New York: Charles Scribner's Sons. 1934.

Belknap, Jeremy. *History of New Hampshire.* 1784-1792.

Bishop, Eugene A. *The Development of a State School System: New Hampshire.* New York: Bureau of Publications, Teachers College, Columbia University. 1930.

Bouton, Nathaniel. *Proceedings of the New Hampshire Historical Society.* 1833. Concord: State Library.

Brown, H. A. *Reports of Inspection of State Normal Schools.* 1913-1917. (Typewritten Bound Reports in the Office of the State Board of Education.)

Buckingham, B. R. *Supply and Demand in Teacher Training.* Bureau of Educational Research Monographs, No. 4. Columbus, Ohio: Ohio State University Studies. 1926.

Bush, George G. *History of Education in New Hampshire.* Circular of Information No. 3. United States Bureau of Education. Washington, D. C.: Government Printing Office. 1898.

Butterfield, E. W. *The State Normal Schools.* Unpublished Report Presented to the State Board of Education. Concord: State Board of Education. 1927.

Butterfield, E. W. *The School Is Just as Good as the Teacher.* Unpublished Report Presented to the State Board of Education, December 6, 1927. Concord: State Board of Education.

Butterfield, E. W. *The Three Reasons.* Unpublished Address Delivered at the New Hampshire State Teachers Association. October 30, 1927.

Butterfield, E. W. *History of New Hampshire Schools and School Legislation. Granite Monthly,* P. G. 57. pp. 19-37. 1925.

Butterfield, E. W. *Recommendations to the Board of Education on Four-Year Courses at the Normal Schools.* Unpublished Report Made December 28, 1925. Concord: State Board of Education.

Butterfield, E. W. *Unpublished Letter to the State Board of Education Re-*

viewing Conference Between the State Board of Education, the Commissioner of Education, and the President of the State University. June 9, 1926. Concord: State Board of Education.

Butterfield, E. W. *Unpublished Letters to the State Board of Education and to the Head of the Department of Education of the University of New Hampshire Concerning Relations of the Department of Education of the University to the Public School System,* August 2 to September 24, 1927. Concord: State Board of Education.

Butterfield, E. W. *Training Teachers for New Hampshire: a Study of the Present Situation and Needs.* Unpublished Report to the State Board of Education, January 17, 1922. Concord: State Board of Education.

Butterfield, E. W. *The Need of Four-Year Curricula at the Normal Schools.* Unpublished Report to the State Board of Education. December 28, 1925. Concord: State Board of Education.

Butterfield, E. W. *New Hampshire's Greatest Need Is Teachers.* Unpublished Report to the State Board of Education, November, 1922. Concord: State Board of Education.

Butterfield, E. W. *The Normal School Situation.* Unpublished Report to the State Board of Education, January 9, 1920. Concord: State Board of Education.

Butterfield, E. W. *The Normal Schools.* Unpublished Address, February 27, 1929. Concord: State Board of Education.

Butterfield, E. W. *The State Normal Schools.* Press Release, September 13, 1927. Concord: State Board of Education.

Butterfield, E. W. *Four-Year Classes.* Unpublished Report to School Board Members. Concord: State Board of Education. 1926.

Butterfield, E. W. *The Training of Teachers for New Hampshire Public Schools.* Unpublished Report to the State Board of Education, January 7, 1922. Concord: State Board of Education.

Catalogs of the State Normal School at Keene. 1908-1934.

Catalogs of the State Normal School at Plymouth. 1871-1934.

Evenden, E. S. *Teacher Supply and Demand in the United States.* Excerpts from *School Life* for January, February, and March, 1931. Washington, D. C.: United States Office of Education.

Folsom, Channing, and Others. *State Grange of New Hampshire.* "Report of the Committee on Education." 1897.

Gordy, J. P. *Rise and Growth of the Normal School Idea in the United States.* Circular of Information, No. 8. Washington, D. C.: Bureau of Education. 1891.

Hall, King S. "Facilities for the Improvement of Teachers." *Ninth Annual Report upon the Schools of New Hampshire,* p. 42. Concord: State Board of Education. 1855.

Hill, C. M. *A Decade of Progress in Teacher Training.* New York: Bureau of Publications, Teachers College, Columbia University. 1931.

Hill, Lawrence B. *The Legislative Control of State Normal Schools.* New York: Bureau of Publications, Teachers College, Columbia University. 1921.

Judd, Charles H. "Teachers Colleges as Centers of Progressive Education."

Yearbook of the American Association of Teachers Colleges. pp. 58-64. 1929.

Judd, Charles H. "The Isolation of the Normal School—Inco-ordination of Administrative Units." *Problems of Education in the United States,* pp. 44-50. New York: McGraw-Hill Book Company. 1933.

Judd, Charles H., and Parker, Samuel C. *Problems Involved In Standardizing State Normal Schools.* Bulletin No. 12., United States Bureau of Education. Washington, D. C.: Government Printing Office. 1916.

Laws of New Hampshire, 1679-1934. Concord: State Board of Education.

Learned, William S., Bagley, William C. and Others. *The Professional Preparation of Teachers for American Public Schools.* Bulletin No. 14, The Carnegie Foundation for the Advancement of Teaching. New York: The Carnegie Foundation. 1920.

McClintock, John N. *History of New Hampshire.* 1888.

Morrison, Henry C. "Does New Hampshire Need a State University?" *The Dartmouth Alumni Magazine,* 6:246-254. May, 1914. Hanover, New Hampshire: Dartmouth College.

Morrison, Henry C. "Economics of Personal Service." *The Management of the School Money,* pp. 233-234. Chicago: The University of Chicago Press. 1931.

Morrison, Henry C. *The College Situation in New England.* Unpublished Address Delivered at the Merrimac Valley Teachers Association, Manchester, New Hampshire. February 20, 1916. Concord: State Board of Education.

Myers, Alonzo F. "Teacher Demand, Supply and Certification." *Yearbook No. XXIII of the National Society of College Teachers of Education,* pp. 186-209. University of Chicago Press. 1935.

Napier, Thomas H. *Trends in the Curricula for Training Teachers.* Peabody Contributions to Education, No. 27. Nashville, Tennessee: George Peabody College for Teachers. 1926.

New Hampshire Normal Schools. *Circular of Information.* "Program of Studies, Curricula and Courses." Concord: State Board of Education. 1933.

New Hampshire State Board of Education. *Regulations Governing the Approval of Superintendents, Head Masters, Principals and Teachers in the Public Schools of New Hampshire.* Concord: State Board of Education. 1934.

Pangburn, Jessie M. *The Evolution of the American Teachers College.* New York: Bureau of Publications, Teachers College, Columbia University. 1932.

Reports of the State Education Department, 1848-1934. Concord: State Board of Education. (Especially reports of Morrison and Butterfield, 1906-1930.)

Sanborn, Edwin D. *History of New Hampshire from Its First Discovery to the Year 1830, with Dissertations, etc. to the Year 1874.* Concord: State Library. 1875.

Simonds, J. W. "Legislative History of Education." *Annual Report of the Superintendent of Public Instruction.* Concord: State Board of Education. 1876.

Stearns, Alfred E., Perry, Lewis and Bill, E. Gordon. *Report of the Committee on New Hampshire Educational Survey.* Concord: State Board of Education. 1929.

Whiton, John M. *Sketches of History of New Hampshire, from Its Settlement in 1823 to 1833.* Concord: State Library, 1834.

VITA

HARRY ALVIN BROWN was born at Liberty, Maine, on August 19, 1879. He received his elementary and secondary education in the schools of the State of Maine, and was graduated from the Maine Central Institute at Pittsfield in 1899. He has received degrees as follows: A.B., Bates College, 1903; A.B., University of Colorado, 1907; A.M., University of Colorado, 1923; Ed.D., Bates College, 1925; Ed.D., Miami University, 1925. He has held the following positions: 1899-1902, teacher in rural schools in Maine; 1903-1904, supervising principal of schools, Liberty, Maine; 1904-1905, district superintendent of schools, Salem, New Hampshire; 1907-1909, city superintendent of schools, Glasgow, Montana; 1909-1913, district superintendent of schools, Colebrook, New Hampshire; 1912, summer session, professor of psychology and education, State Normal School, Plymouth, New Hampshire; 1913-1917, assistant commissioner of education and director of educational research, State Department of Education, Concord, New Hampshire; 1916, summer session, professor of education, State Normal School, Keene, New Hampshire; 1921, summer session, associate professor of education, University of Chicago; 1922-1926, member of committee on standards and chairman in 1925-1926, American Association of Teachers Colleges; 1917-1930, president of the State Teachers College, Oshkosh, Wisconsin; 1931, summer session, professor of education, State Normal School, Keene, New Hampshire; 1930-1933, president of the Illinois State Normal University; 1932-1933, president of the American Association of Teachers Colleges; 1933-1934, consultant in teacher education, Connecticut State Board of Education; 1934—, superintendent of schools, Needham, Massachusetts. During the winter and spring sessions of 1933-1934 and the June and summer sessions of 1934, he was a graduate student at Teachers College, Columbia University, in teacher education and philosophy of education. He has written a number of articles and monographs, among which the following are the most important:

A Study of Ability in Latin in Secondary Schools. Concord, New Hampshire: State Education Department. iv + 170 pp. 1919.

"Some Next Steps in Establishing Standards for Teachers Colleges." *Elementary School Journal,* 25: 211-216. November, 1924. (Also in Yearbook of the American Association of Teachers Colleges. pp. 43-57, 1924.)

"What Should Wisconsin Normal Schools do Before They Grant Degrees?" *Educational Administration and Supervision,* 12: 353-412. September, 1926.

"On What Should Teachers Colleges Place Chief Emphasis in Developing Higher Standards?" *Yearbook of the American Association of Teachers Colleges,* 45-57. 1926.

"Some Next Steps in the Preparation of Teachers." *Educational Administration and Supervision,* 17: 161-180. March, 1931.

"Building a Profession of Education through Improved Teacher Preparation." *School and Society,* 33: 546-556. April 25, 1931.

"Some Unsolved Problems of Teacher Preparation." *Yearbook of the American Association of Teachers Colleges,* 95-109. 1931.

"Elements in Effective Teacher Education." *The Illinois Teacher,* 21: 79-81 and 104-106. November and December, 1932.

"The Redirection of Teacher Education." *Annual Report of the Department of Superintendence of the National Education Association.* 68-75. Washington, D. C.: The Department of Superintendence of the National Education Association. 1933.

"An Experiment in Organizing Courses in Education for Elementary School Teachers." *Educational Administration and Supervision,* 19: 451-462. September, 1933.

"Essential Constituents of a Program for the Preparation of Elementary School Teachers," in *Problems in Teacher Training.* Proceedings of the 1933 Spring Conference of the Eastern States Association of Professional Schools for Teachers, 8: 140-159. 1933.

"Reformulation of Theory and Practice in Teacher Education." *Journal of Higher Education,* 5: 490-496. December, 1934.

"Improved Teacher Education as a Basis for Better Teaching." *Education,* 57: 367-373. February, 1937.

DATE DUE